WISDOM
AT WORK

WISDOM AT WORK

A BIBLICAL APPROACH TO THE WORKPLACE

KENNETH
BOA
&
GAIL
BURNETT

NAVPRESS

BRINGING TRUTH TO LIFE
P.O. Box 35001, Colorado Springs, Colorado 80935

OUR GUARANTEE TO YOU

We believe so strongly in the message of our books that we are making this quality guarantee to you. If for any reason you are disappointed with the content of this book, return the title page to us with your name and address and we will refund to you the list price of the book. To help us serve you better, please briefly describe why you were disappointed. Mail your refund request to: NavPress, P.O. Box 35002, Colorado Springs, CO 80935.

The Navigators is an international Christian organization. Our mission is to reach, disciple, and equip people to know Christ and to make Him known through successive generations. We envision multitudes of diverse people in the United States and every other nation who have a passionate love for Christ, live a lifestyle of sharing Christ's love, and multiply spiritual laborers among those without Christ.

NavPress is the publishing ministry of The Navigators. NavPress publications help believers learn biblical truth and apply what they learn to their lives and ministries. Our mission is to stimulate spiritual formation among our readers.

Cover photo by Masterfile/Roy Ooms
Cover design by Dan Jamison
Creative Team: Steve Webb, Darla Hightower, Tim Howard, Melissa Munro

Some of the anecdotal illustrations in this book are true-to-life and are included with the permission of the persons involved. All other illustrations are composites of real situations, and any resemblance to people living or dead is coincidental.

Unless otherwise identified, all Scripture quotations in this publication are taken from the *New American Standard Bible* (NASB), © The Lockman Foundation 1960, 1962, 1963, 1968, 1971, 1972, 1973, 1975, 1977, 1995, 1997. In some instances, italics and font formatting have been altered in the Scripture verses. Other versions include: the King James Version (KJV); the HOLY BIBLE: NEW INTERNATIONAL VERSION (NIV), Copyright 1973, 1978, 1984 by Zondervan Publishing House, all rights reserved.

Boa, Kenneth.
    Wisdom at work : a biblical approach to the workplace / Kenneth Boa &
    Gail Burnett.
        p. cm.
    ISBN 1-57683-197-3
    1. Work—Religious aspects—Christianity—Biblical teaching. I. Burnett,
Gail. II. Title.
    BS680.W75 B63 2000
    248.8'8--dc21   00-026742
                                                                        CIP

Printed in the United States of America

1 2 3 4 5 6 7 8 9 10 11 12 13 14 15 / 01 00 99

TABLE OF CONTENTS

ACKNOWLEDGMENTS   6

AS YOU STUDY   7

HOW TO USE THIS GUIDEBOOK   8

INTRODUCTION—WISDOM AT WORK   9

INTRODUCTION TO UNIT 1: WORK—IS IT PLEASURE OR PAIN?   11
Day 1: What Is Work? (Part 1)   12
Day 2: What Is Work? (Part 2)   14
Day 3: Work as God Intended It   16
Day 4: The Curse and the Nature of Work   20
Day 5: Hope for Redeeming Our Work   24

INTRODUCTION TO UNIT 2: CHOOSING OUR WORK   29
Day 1: Is Work Optional?   30
Day 2: Career: Choice or Calling?   34
Day 3: Career: Secular or Spiritual?   38
Day 4: Does Money Matter?   42
Day 5: What Is Our Spiritual Calling?   46

INTRODUCTION TO UNIT 3: WORK AND IDENTITY   51
Day 1: Seeking Significance in Giftedness   52
Day 2: Seeking Significance in Education   56
Day 3: Seeking Significance in Profession   60
Day 4: Seeking Significance in Power   64
Day 5: Finding Significance in Service   68

INTRODUCTION TO UNIT 4: WORK AND WEALTH   73
Day 1: Work and Profit   74
Day 2: Work and Prosperity   78
Day 3: Work and Provision   82
Day 4: Work and Wages   86
Day 5: Work and Abundance   90

INTRODUCTION TO UNIT 5: WORK AND CHARACTER   95
Day 1: Attributes of God's Employees   96
Day 2: Attitudes of God's Employees   100
Day 3: Mentoring God's Employees   104
Day 4: Human Relations and God's Employees   108
Day 5: Spiritual Riches of God's Employees   112

APPENDIX A: SCRIPTURE READINGS   117

APPENDIX B: GOD'S PLAN OF SALVATION   137

APPENDIX C: ADDITIONAL ROAD MAP SCRIPTURE REFERENCES   141

ACKNOWLEDGMENTS

I (Gail) cannot write about the workplace without thinking of my own career and of my personal appreciation for all those who have helped me along the way. Many thanks to Dr. Larry Zechman, Conard Stair, and Ken Sommerfeld, my first workplace encouragers. (How I wish I had been mature enough to have borne more fruit!) And special thanks to my patient attorney and dear friend, Jim Tipton, and to my much-loved mentor, Bob Hedrick.

AS YOU STUDY

Spiritual maturity begins with a diligent study of the Word of God. The more you take in and live out, the more you grow in Christlikeness. There's no substitute for spending time in the Word. Time, however, is a diminishing resource in our complex society; and schedules are rarely routine for anyone.

To help address these issues, Dr. Boa and I have developed what we call the GUIDEBOOK series. Guided tours carry people to places of interest, providing information from experts along the way. People take guided tours for a number of reasons. Sometimes they don't know where to go. Sometimes they want more information. Sometimes their time is limited. Sometimes their understanding is limited. In all cases, they need a guidebook.

The GUIDEBOOK series is aptly named. The workbooks are vehicles and we (your tour guides) are longtime Bible teachers and writers. Dr. Boa, in fact, is a theological expert. As we guide you through the themes of choosing our work, work and identity, work and wealth, and work and character, we'll be drawing your attention to key passages in Scripture. These passages are significant because of their relationship to something of greater importance; namely, God's plan of salvation.

To help you get the most out of your journey, read the suggestions in the adjacent column before you go on. We hope you'll enjoy *Wisdom at Work*. Now, buckle your seat belt. We're ready to go!

—Gail Burnett

GETTING THE MOST FROM YOUR STUDY

1. **Begin with prayer.** You can gain information on your own, but only God can reveal truth.
2. **Do not read commentaries on this material until you have finished the entire study.** Self-discovery of biblical truth is exciting. It makes the Word of God come alive and also helps you retain what you've learned.
3. **Make sure you understand the structure of this GUIDEBOOK before you begin.** (Explanations are found on the following page.)
4. **Do not skip over directions to read the referenced Scriptures.** The text that follows may not make sense if you have not first read the Scripture passage(s).
5. **Be sure to write your answers to the study questions in the space provided.** Repetition and space for content interaction have been included to help you retain the material. Your answers will be confirmed in subsequent readings. These answers are intended to reinforce what you've already read and written.
6. **Work on this study every day of the week.** Begin the first day of your study week by reading the "unit introduction" page. Work through the Daily Excursions over the next five days, then end your week with review and Scripture memory. You may want to preview "Sharing the Journey" if you are using this study with a group.
7. **Read the articles and suggested Daily Readings in the optional Side Tours, even if you don't have time to do the activities.** The articles and readings are important, and they can be read in a few minutes.
8. **During your day, meditate on what you've learned.** Most Daily Excursions can be completed in less than twenty minutes, but they are "tightly packed." Reflecting on your observations allows biblical truths to expand your understanding and to take shape in your life.

HOW TO USE THIS GUIDEBOOK

INSTRUCTIONAL DESIGN©

GUIDEBOOKS are self-contained, interactive Bible studies. These studies are primarily inductive; that is, they lead the reader to related Scriptures throughout the Bible so that he or she might experience the joy of self-discovery as revealed by the Master Himself. Therefore, in addition to Scripture references from the key texts, topics are supported by the whole counsel of God. Other outside material and additional Scripture references are included in "For further study."

Each GUIDEBOOK includes five study units divided into five **Daily Excursions**. Most Excursions take about twenty minutes to complete. No additional reference materials are needed. To complete the optional Side Tours, a Bible and a concordance are sometimes needed.

PAGE DESCRIPTION

GUIDEBOOKS are designed for open, two-page viewing. Each page is divided into two columns—a wide inside column and a narrow outside column, as shown below. Daily Excursions include Bible teaching, related questions, life application (Bringing It Home), and Bible reading. The outside columns contain related Road Map and Side Tour options. At the end of each unit, it is suggested that the reader select one verse from the weekly reading to memorize.

The **Road Map** includes all Bible verses referred to in the Daily Excursions, except for lengthy study texts. (These are provided in appendix A). Scriptures in the Road Map are linked to reference numbers in the Daily Excursions and numbered consecutively throughout the GUIDEBOOK. Unless otherwise noted, all Scripture passages are from the *New American Standard Bible,* Updated Edition.

Within quoted Scriptures, ellipses (. . .) indicate where portions of text have been omitted (due to space constraints) without compromising the meaning. The verses provided include the essential information for your study; however, you will benefit from reading the full text from your Bible.

The **Side Tours** contain optional reading and Scripture references related to Language & Literature, History & Culture, Bible Study Techniques, Cross References, Scripture Meditation, and Points of Interest (including life illustrations). All Side Tours are referenced in the text and numbered consecutively (preceded by "T") throughout the GUIDEBOOK. For example, the notation [T1] will follow the appropriate text in the Daily Excursion, and this same notation will appear in the adjacent Side Tour column. Because the Scriptures listed in Side Tours are not printed in this GUIDEBOOK, they must be looked up in a Bible.

Personal experiences of the authors are differentiated by their names in parentheses.

ROAD MAP	DAILY EXCURSION
	DAY 1
	EXAMINING PROVERBS AS LITERATURE
¹PROVERBS 1	
1 The proverbs [mashal] of Solomon the son of David, king of Israel:	What defines a proverb? The Hebrew word for "proverb" is transliterated[T1] *mashal*, which means "a discourse or a parable." *Mashal* comes from a root word that means "to
2 To know wisdom and instruction, To discern the sayings of understanding,	be similar or parallel; to represent; to be like or be compared to." The book of Proverbs uses comparisons as
3 To receive instruction in wise behavior. Righteousness	

DAILY EXCURSION	SIDE TOURS
BRINGING IT HOME . . .	**HISTORY & CULTURE:[T3]**
1. Look back at your life—as a child, a teen, and a young adult. Also look at your life now. At what point, if any, did you make a choice to reject being naive and foolish and to embrace wisdom? In what ways does that choice still impact your life today?	AUTHORSHIP—King Solomon, son of David, did not write all of the proverbs, but his work makes up the greater part of the book. Solomon was an observer and a seeker of knowledge. Not only was Solomon's knowledge encyclopedic, his understanding and discernment were such that his

INTRODUCTION—WISDOM AT WORK

There are, no doubt, more job titles in America than anyplace else in the world. We do all kinds of work—some we like and some we don't. And we have a tremendous vocabulary to describe our work. We Americans work like horses, work like dogs, and work like slaves. We work our fingers to the bone, keep our noses to the grindstone, and put our shoulders to the wheel. We pound away, plug along, and buckle down until we are overdriven, over-tasked, overtaxed, and overburdened. For our arduous, onerous, and wearisome labors we receive hard-fought, hard-earned dollars—our reward for giving the sweat of our brow, with might and main, tooth and nail, heart and soul. We leave work fatigued, bone weary, worn out, used up, pooped, bushed, frazzled, spent, exhausted, and just plumb tuckered out.

This melodrama is quite amusing—and amazing, considering few of us even break a sweat in the course of our normal workday. Nevertheless, this small sampling of an incredible number of work-related words, phrases, and idioms is an indicator of how important work is in our lives. This sampling also reveals how often we view our work in a negative light.

That we have many negative terms relating to our work is hardly surprising. Few people express real satisfaction with their jobs, regardless of their careers or professions. But because most of us will spend more than one hundred thousand hours in the workplace, it is in our best interest to examine work issues through the lens of God's Word. This is the reason we have written this study.

Wisdom at Work will guide you to Scriptures throughout the Bible that deal with work issues common to our experience. Our goal as teachers is to help you reexamine your work as a means of worship so that you might leverage your labor to the glory of God. May your workplace become an arena for your growth and His glory.

INTRODUCTION TO UNIT 1
WORK—IS IT PLEASURE OR PAIN?

Destination: To gain an understanding of work from a biblical perspective.

Before I began writing today, I (Gail) wanted to get a few chores out of the way. I made some calls, faxed materials to a Christian ministry, paid a bill, attended to a few housekeeping responsibilities, ran a couple of quick errands, and made lunch. When I sat down at the computer, I thought, *I'm already tired, and I haven't even started to work!*

Observing this scenario objectively, I realize, of course, that I had been working for several hours already. But, like most people in our Western culture, I tend to view "work" as synonymous with "job," and "job" as synonymous with "the activity that provides my livelihood." Only under someone else's employment would I have thought of those administrative and domestic duties as "real" work (a notion that is particularly and rightly irksome to moms and homemakers).

Tasks that define work can be hard to pin down. One person sews for a clothing manufacturer, and that's work. Another person sews for a hobby, so it's leisure. One person chisels rock in a quarry, and that's work. Another chisels stone in her basement, and it's art. Even in income-producing environments, work can be a slippery concept. Suppose a man loves his job and finds great enjoyment and fulfillment in performing it. Is he working in the same way as another man who performs the same duties simply for financial survival and loathes every minute of it?

What exactly is work?[1] Is work a blessing or a curse? Do we want to work, or do we want work to just go away? Beyond basic provision, does work have any higher purpose, or is work simply a source of pain, a punishment inherited from Adam and Eve's rebellion? In this GUIDEBOOK study, we'll be looking at our work worlds from God's perspective, using His Word to answer these and other important questions.

As you work through unit 1, you will unfold a multifaceted concept of work as presented in Scripture. If unit 1 seems a bit academic to you, just keep in mind that you are building an important foundation from which to more knowledgeably examine Scriptures on workplace issues.

As you begin this study, apply the exhortation from 2 Timothy 2:15: "Be diligent to present yourself approved to God as a workman who does not need to be ashamed, accurately handling the word of truth."

---

[1] Scientists who study work issues use precise, technical definitions that make distinctions among work-related terms such as *job, task, occupation, profession, vocation,* and so on. In this study, however, we use these terms somewhat interchangeably, as in everyday speech.

¹**DEUTERONOMY 26**

6-7 The Egyptians treated us harshly and afflicted us, and imposed hard labor *[abodah]* on us. Then we cried to the LORD, the God of our fathers, and the LORD heard our voice and saw our affliction and our toil *[amal]* and our oppression.

DAY 1

WHAT IS WORK? (PART 1)

It seems strange to ask, "What is work?" Work, we may think, is simply a given, an inseparable component of both individual and community responsibility. Work is so commonplace in our lives that few of us spend time pondering its purpose, much less analyzing its impact on our lives and our culture. But our work is important—to us, to our society, and to God.

Social scientists tell us that there is a relationship between the importance of a cultural concept or issue and the number of words coined to describe it.[T1] Certainly this is true of work in our society. Americans have coined a remarkable number of English words (including slang) that not only allow us to refer specifically to our work but also to simultaneously describe how we *feel* about it.

Below is a short list of work-related terms. Beside each of these terms, indicate with a plus (+) if the word resonates positively with you or a minus (-) if the word has a negative feel.

Work-Related Terms

accomplish	administer	build	bring forth
clean	construct	conduct	craft
create	cultivate	design	develop
fix	grind	labor	maintain
make	minister	operate	organize
oversee	perform	plod	pound
produce	sell	serve	slave
supervise	toil	weary	work

This tiny sampling of words that define or describe work is an indicator of how deeply work issues are woven into the fabric of our lives. Obviously, our work is important to us; nevertheless, we often refer to it negatively. Does anyone really enjoy his or her work? Do you enjoy the work involved in your primary job? Mark your own degree of personal satisfaction with your work experience using the Employment Enjoyment Scale that follows:

Employment Enjoyment Scale

1___ 2___ 3___ 4___ 5__ 6___ 7___ 8___ 9___ 10___
Miserable   Very Enjoyable

"WORK" IN BIBLE LANGUAGES

Neither Hebrew and Aramaic (the languages of the Old Testament) nor Greek (the language of the New Testament) provide as many verbal tools for describing work activities as does English. Nevertheless, these languages offer enough words to make important differentiations among types of work activities. And shades of meaning are further discernible by the immediate context.[T2]

Read Deuteronomy 26:6-7[1] from the Road Map column. Select some words from the list of work-related terms that best convey the apparent meaning of the following Hebrew words, based solely on the context.

abodah:

amal:

When describing these words, did you select more positive (+) or more negative (-) words?

What employment enjoyment score (from the scale on page 12) might you give to *abodah* and *amal*? _____

Abodah specifically refers to service or labor that is imposed or forced on a group, typically slaves. *Amal* means "heavy toil; labor that is associated with anguish or involves suffering." In the *New American Standard Bible,* Updated Edition (used as the primary text in this course), *abodah* is translated "hard labor" and *amal* is translated "toil."

There is no question that the type of effort described in these two Hebrew words constitutes real work. Both of these words convey not only physical labor but also labor in the harshest of terms.

As you conclude today's study, think of contemporary activities that might be described by *abodah* or *amal*.

Would you include agricultural work as *abodah* or as *amal*? Why?

(*Note:* We will be looking at Adam's agricultural work in this unit, so keep your answer in mind.)

LANGUAGE & LIT:[T1]

ARE WE VERBALLY COLOR-BLIND?—Social scientists tell us that in every culture there is a relationship between the value of a concept and the number of words that are coined to distinguish among its features. People who live on tropical islands, for example, have more words to distinguish between various shades of blue than do people who live inland. Similarly, Eskimo languages have more words to distinguish between types of snow than does our English language. This is significant in each of those cultures because those subtle variations might signal to islanders or Eskimos that serious weather is in store.

That language reflects (or perhaps even defines) human perception is a fascinating concept. If such a correlation exists, we should consider those concepts that we claim to highly praise but have coined relatively few distinguishing synonyms or adjectives to describe. For example, how many synonyms do you know for "love"?

LANGUAGE & LIT:[T2]

CONTEXT—Context is one of the key components to understanding a Scripture passage. The immediate context is determined by the way the words or sentences fit sensibly with the text surrounding it. Historical context refers to the broader issues that help determine the purpose of the writing. These include the author, the recipients, the time period, the culture, and so on. A Bible dictionary or Bible encyclopedia is a good place to find answers to questions concerning historical context. These are available at your local Christian bookstore, or perhaps in your church library.

[2] **OLD TESTAMENT**

Genesis 29:22 Laban gathered all the men of the place, and made [asah] a feast.

Genesis 31:1 From what belonged to our father he [Jacob] has made [asah] all this wealth.

Genesis 47:3 Pharaoh said . . . "What is your occupation [maaseh]?" So they said to Pharaoh, "Your servants are shepherds."

Exodus 20:11 In six days the LORD made [asah] the heavens and the earth.

Exodus 28:6 They shall also make [asah] the ephod of gold, of blue and purple and scarlet material and fine twisted linen, the work [maaseh] of the skillful workman.

1 Chronicles 5:10 In the days of Saul they made [asah] war with the Hagrites.

Psalm 102:25 Of old You founded the earth, And the heavens are the work [maaseh] of Your hands.

[3] **NEW TESTAMENT**

Luke 5:5 Simon answered and said, "Master, we worked hard [kopiao] all night and caught nothing."

John 4:34 Jesus said to them, "My food is to do the will of Him who sent Me and to accomplish His work [ergon]."

John 9:4 "We must work [ergazomai] the works [ergon] of Him who sent Me as long as it is day; night is coming when no man can work [ergazomai]."

Ephesians 4:11-12 He gave some as apostles . . . evangelists, and . . . pastors and teachers, for the equipping of the saints for the work [ergon] of service. . . .

Ephesians 4:28 He who steals must steal no longer; but rather he must labor [ergazomai], performing with his own hands what is good. . . .

DAY 2

WHAT IS WORK? (PART 2)

On day 1 we discussed the large number of English words that define various types of work and work-related ideas. We also looked at two Hebrew words that identified work involving heavy toil, forced labor, and anguish.

In today's session, we want to look at two more Hebrew words for "work"—*asah* and its derivative *maaseh*. Read the selected excerpts from the Old Testament.[2] As in our last excursion, use words from the list of work-related terms (page 12) that seem to most closely convey what these Hebrew words mean, based solely on the context.

asah:

maaseh:

Do these terms for work seem more appealing than *amal* and *abodah*? On average, how would you score the enjoyment potential of *asah* and *maaseh*? ____

Asah refers to work that makes, produces, builds, or creates something—from books to banquets to battles. *Asah* means "to take action; to accomplish; to bring forth." The word is also used of people's response to God's commands, and it applies specifically to *all* His acts and actions.

Maaseh (derived from *asah*) refers to the finished product of the worker, that is, to his achievements. *Melakah*, a synonym of *maaseh*, is probably the Hebrew word closest in meaning to the English words "job," "occupation," and "vocation."

There are several other Hebrew words for "work," but these four—*amal* and *abodah* (from yesterday's study) plus *asah* and its derivative *maaseh*—are the most frequently used words for "work" in the Old Testament.

GREEK WORDS FOR "WORK"

In Greek, the most frequently used words for "work" are *kopiao* and *ergon* (in their various forms). Read the excerpts of New Testament references[3] and determine from the context which words in the list of work-related terms (page 12) most closely define *kopiao*.

kopiao:

What is the Hebrew equivalent of *kopiao*?

Kopiao means "hard labor; weariness; toil." It comes from the root word *kopos,* which means "trouble and misery." Bilingual Jews who translated the Old Testament into Greek (284–247 B.C.)[T3] selected the word *kopiao* as the Greek substitute for the Hebrew word *amal.*

The second primary Greek word that is translated "work," *ergon* (and its noun form *ergazomai*) means "work, deeds, or business activities that are directed toward a goal." *Ergon's* meaning most closely parallels the Hebrew words *asah* and *maaseh.*

Why have we looked so intently at word meanings? First, if we're going to be looking at work from God's perspective, then we have to let Scripture (not the English dictionary) define our terms. Second, we must examine key words and their root words from their language of origin (rather than from an English translation) to gain insight into their fuller meaning.[T4] From the meaning of *ergon* we now know, for example, that work will expend energy. We know from both *asah* and *ergon* that the energy of work must be directed toward some goal, task, or performance. We also know from the definitions of *kopiao, amal,* and *abodah* that some kinds of work will be forced labor and will involve suffering or anguish.

BRINGING IT HOME

1. The studies on days 1 and 2 have probably seemed a bit technical. The purpose of these exercises, however, is to free you from culturally imposed, twentieth-century work concepts and to help you better understand work issues from Scripture.

   Choose five words from the work-related terms on page 12 that best describe your own job. Are these words more positive (+), more negative (-), or neutral? Compare these descriptions with the score you gave on the Employment Enjoyment Scale, page 12. Are the two in agreement? Why or why not? Ask God to open up your understanding so that you might get a new perspective on the meaning of work.

HISTORY & CULTURE:[T3]

THE SEPTUAGINT—The books of the Old Testament were written over a long period of time. Some of the books may have been collected under the reign of King Solomon (970–930 B.C.). Other books were added as the people of Israel experienced and documented great blessings or great trouble. Among the crises brought on by national corruption, as revealed in the books of the prophets, were the conquests of Israel by other nations and the resulting dispersion of the Jews into other lands.

By the time Rome conquered the Greeks, Jews were scattered throughout the empire. Most spoke Greek, and all but a few had forgotten the ancient Hebrew language. From 284–247 B.C., a few bilingual Jews translated the Hebrew Scriptures into Greek. This Greek translation of the Old Testament, known as the Septuagint, established the order of the thirty-nine Old Testament books as we use them today. The Septuagint also contains other Jewish writings often referred to as the Apocrypha. As these writings were not part of the original books of Scripture, however, they are not included in the sacred canon of the Old Testament.

STUDY TECHNIQUES:[T4]

WORD STUDIES—Language is dynamic; that is, it evolves to reflect new developments in the culture. The noun *computer,* for example, evolved from the verb "to compute," reflecting the mathematical process of a computer's operating system.

When we study Scripture, we always look up the "root" words from which other words are derived. Finding the meanings of words of origin greatly expands our understanding of Scripture.

17-19 Cursed is the ground because of you; in toil you will eat of it all the days of your life. Both thorns and thistles it shall grow for you; and you shall eat the plants of the field; by the sweat of your face you will eat bread.

[5] **GENESIS 1 & 2**
1:31 God saw all that He had made, and behold, it was very good.
2:9 Out of the ground the LORD God caused to grow every tree that is pleasing to the sight and good for food.

[6] **ISAIAH 51**
3 Indeed, the LORD will comfort Zion. . . . And her wilderness He will make like Eden, and her desert like the garden of the LORD; joy and gladness will be found in her, thanksgiving and sound of a melody.

[7] **GENESIS 2**
4-9,15 This is the account of the heavens and the earth when they were created. . . . Now no shrub of the field was yet in the earth, and no plant of the field had yet sprouted, for the LORD God had not sent rain upon the earth; and there was no man to cultivate the ground. . . . Then the LORD God formed man of dust from the ground, and breathed into his nostrils the breath of life; and man became a living being. The LORD God planted a garden toward the east, in Eden. . . . Then the LORD God took the man and put him into the garden of Eden to cultivate it and keep it.

DAY 3

WORK AS GOD INTENDED IT

The purpose of work is the subject of much debate by thinkers in various fields, from sociology to economics to theology. Many Christians (and some non-Christians) think that work is the punishment we all inherited as a result of Adam's sin. We'll examine this idea more closely in today's study. Begin by quickly scanning Genesis 1–3 from appendix A.

Now let's analyze some of these selected verses. From the Road Map column, read about God's response to Adam's sin from Genesis 3:17-19.[4] Specifically, what was cursed as a result of Adam's disobedience?

How was this curse to be manifested?

Let's back up a bit. From the description of the curse, what conclusions might be drawn about the garden prior to Adam and Eve's rebellion?

From nothing tangible, God created "stuff," including a garden that must have been lavish. The Garden of Eden is often referred to as a place of perfection, though Genesis doesn't say so explicitly. How, then, do we know? Read the verses from Genesis 1 and 2[5] in the Road Map column. How did God characterize all that He had made?

Part of our understanding of perfection comes from knowing that God's work is always perfect. Also, the meaning of the Hebrew word for "good" (*tob*) paints a clearer picture of perfection than does the English translation. *Tob* means "abundantly pleasant; exceedingly pleasing." *Tob* is also translated "beautiful, charming, cheerful, delightful, safe, sound, worthy."

We have glimpses into Eden from other Scriptures as well.[T5] Genesis 13:10, for example, tells us the garden of the Lord was well watered. From Ezekiel 31:8 and 28:13 we learn that Eden contained cedars, cypresses, and plane trees as well as an abundance of precious stones.

God's garden was more than just physically beautiful. Read Isaiah 51:3.[6] From the comparisons provided by this verse, what do we learn about Eden's atmosphere? Draw a symbol that, for you, conveys the mood that must have existed in the Garden of Eden.

Now, read of God's plan and provision for Adam in Genesis 2:4-9,15.[7] What was Adam's responsibility in the Garden of Eden? Was this before or after he sinned?

Adam and Eve lived in a beautiful environment that fostered a sense of well-being. We can rightly conclude, therefore, that Eden knew no *amal* or *abodah*—no heavy toil, no slavery, no frustration. Nevertheless, from the beginning God had designed a garden that would be dependent upon a steward. In that design, He created a job for Adam before He created Adam himself. Why do you think God did this? Check the reason that you think comes closest to the truth.

___ God couldn't keep the garden Himself.
___ God wanted to create busy work for Adam.
___ God knew work would be fulfilling for Adam.

Adam and Eve's assignments were to take the earth's raw materials and begin nurturing, organizing, and shaping them into something useful—a creative task intended to give each of them purpose and pleasure. Read Isaiah 28:23-26.[8] How did Adam learn his job skills? That is, how did he know how to cultivate and care for God's garden?

Review the Scriptures relating to God's garden at Creation and His initial plans for humanity. Do you think Adam's assignments before the curse constituted "real" work? If not, why not? If so, was it *asah* or *amal?*

Your answer probably relates to your own definition of work. And, as we mentioned in the introduction, work can be difficult to define.

STUDY TECHNIQUES:[T5]

CROSS-REFERENCING—When studying a topic in the Bible, we want to find the full counsel of God before taking a theological position. We accomplish this in a couple of different ways.

Most Bibles have cross-reference notations directly in the text. These superscript letters or numbers are keyed to a matching letter or number located in the small column that (in most cases) runs either down the inside margin of each page or the center of the page. Notations here identify other passages in Scripture where the subject is also discussed.

While these cross-references are helpful, they are usually not exhaustive. A more thorough study can be accomplished with a concordance (see "Language & Lit: More on Word Studies," page 21). When looking up a topic in a concordance, be sure to include synonyms.

SCRIPTURE MEDITATION

Look for a Scripture passage at the end of each Daily Excursion. Meditate on this Scripture throughout your day, asking yourself, *How does this passage apply to my work life?* Consider memorizing the verses of your Scripture Meditation.

Here's today's Scripture Meditation: "I know how to get along with humble means, and I also know how to live in prosperity; in any and every circumstance I have learned the secret of being filled and going hungry, both of having abundance and suffering need. I can do all things through Him who strengthens me" (Philippians 4:12-13).

[8]**ISAIAH 28**

23-26 Give ear and hear my voice, listen and hear my words. Does the farmer plow continually to plant seed? Does he continually turn and harrow the ground? Does he not level its surface, and sow dill and scatter cummin, and plant wheat in rows, barley in its place, and rye within its area? For his God instructs and teaches him properly.

[9]**GENESIS 1**

26-28 Then God said, "Let Us make man in Our image, according to Our likeness; and let them rule over the fish of the sea and over the birds of the sky and over the cattle and over all the earth, and over every creeping thing that creeps on the earth." God created man in His own image, in the image of God He created him; male and female He created them. God blessed them; and God said to them, "Be fruitful and multiply, and fill the earth, and subdue it; and rule over the fish of the sea and over the birds of the sky, and over every living thing that moves on the earth."

Let's assume for the moment that "work" is synonymous with "job." What elements do you think would be necessary to make one's work pleasurable or enjoyable? Briefly note your ideas of the "perfect" job as you, personally, would envision it.

In the Garden of Eden, both Adam and Eve held power positions. They could order and shape their own world and, in doing so, both subdue and serve it. Adam and Eve's work had meaning—theirs were not irrelevant tasks. Both were trained in horticulture and animal husbandry by the Head of the universe; they received from Him all the knowledge, wisdom, and strength they needed to carry out their duties with full vigor and confidence. And both enjoyed unlimited opportunities for creative expression.

In addition, the earth and all it contained were subject to Adam and Eve's authority. They served as vicegerents (managing rulers), administering duties under the Great King. And their compensation was all the fullness of a lush and bountiful land. Based on this description, would you consider Adam and Eve's job a blessing or a curse? Why?

Most of us think a job like Adam's would be *heavenly*—and we'd be right! There was something heavenly not only about the job but also about Adam and Eve themselves. Read Genesis 1:26-28.[9] Who served as the model for humankind at Creation? For which gender?

Both Adam and Eve reflected the image of their Creator; thus they shared some of His attributes. Read Genesis 1:26-28 again. Select single verbs that describe God's work and Adam and Eve's duties and write them below:

<u>God's Work</u>　　　　<u>Adam & Eve's Duties</u>

God worked by speaking, making, creating, and blessing His creation. Check each word on the next page that might describe God's motivation to work (to create the cosmos and man).

__coercion   __*asah*   __drudgery   __voluntary
__satisfaction   __*amal*   __joy   __self-expression

Adam and Eve were told to "be," "fill," "rule," and "subdue." Go back and circle each word in the previous list that describes what you think might have motivated Adam to do the work God initially had given him.

If we understand that God delighted in His creative work and that He created human beings to share in His image and likeness, then we realize that work was a marvelous gift from God. It is reasonable to believe—indeed, it is hard *not* to believe—that work was given *before the Fall* to meet the human need for purpose and creative expression, and that is a need that goes far deeper than mere self-preservation.

The desire to work, then, was ignited by a divine spark that drew both Adam and Eve into creative activities. Nothing else they could do would reflect the image of their Creator more than this for, even today, it is human creativity that sets men and women apart from every other living thing on this planet.[T6]

BRINGING IT HOME

1. Close your eyes for a moment and try to imagine one day of total freedom from work (remember to include all creative activities as well as all unpleasant tasks). If the idea appeals to you, also imagine someone else doing even your personal chores—fixing your hair, changing your TV channels, reading your paper. Now, multiply that day into a week and that week into months and years of nonproductive activity. Do these thoughts elicit any emotional response? What is it?

2. Based on the things you've learned so far, write a biblical definition of work. As you work at your job this week, pay attention to elements of your work that reflect your definition. (Be prepared to modify your definition as you proceed through this study.)

POINT OF INTEREST:[T6]

CREATIVE DIRECTOR—"Do you know where cars come from?" my young grandson, Haden, asked.

"Well, not exactly," I (Gail) answered truthfully. "Do you?"

"Yes," he said in his most authoritative voice. "God made 'em."

I stammered before I began the not-so-easy task of explaining to a five year old the difference between what God has made and what people have recycled.

"Yes, God made the raw materials," I began. "God made rocks in the ground with iron in them. People dig out the rocks, melt out the iron, mix it with something called carbon, and make steel. That's the metal that's shaped into a car. God made pockets of oil and natural gas in the earth. People tap into these pockets and make fuel to run the cars. God also made rubber trees and fibrous plants. People harvest them to make tires. And God puts the knowledge of how to make all those things in our minds.

"So really, Haden," I concluded, "a car is made by God working with and through people. So when *you* make something from God's raw materials, God will be working with you, too, as your Partner."

Haden's eyes widened as the idea of God's partnership penetrated his thoughts. But in the telling I, too, was gripped by the truth that the almighty God is Himself working with us and in us and through us, mentoring us, being our partner, and guiding the work of our hands. No wonder He tells us to come to Him in awe and wonder—just like a child.

DAY 4

THE CURSE AND THE NATURE OF WORK

Work was meant to be a perpetual source of fascination and blessing for Adam and Eve. Sin, however, changed the nature of work because God's curse changed the nature of nature. We saw in Genesis 3:17-19[4] that the ground (*adamah*) was cursed because of Adam's sin. Read Genesis 5:29[10] and Romans 8:19-22.[11] Check the phrase that best describes the extent of the curse, according to these verses.

___ Confined to the Garden of Eden
___ Encompassing the whole earth
___ Encompassing the entire cosmos
___ Confined to Adam's personal garden

To what was all of creation enslaved?

According to Romans 8, the entire cosmos was enslaved to corruption, and it continues to groan in anguish over its own condition. Why do you think the whole earth had to be cursed when humankind was cursed?

Fallen humanity could not retain dominion over an otherwise perfect creation. When Adam was evicted from God's garden, he immediately began to experience the human conflict with an unruly, unresponsive world. The curse changed Adam's environment from a place of safety, security, and satisfying work to a place most uncooperative and sometimes hostile. In a corrupted environment, then, Adam's work became difficult, frustrating, even frightening.

WORK WITHOUT ETERNAL PURPOSE

Read Romans 8:19-22 again. To what was creation unwillingly subjected?

The Greek word for "futility" is *mataios,* from the root word *mate,* meaning "in vain, to no purpose, empty." As a purposeful and useful creation was subjected to futility, so was the work of people's hands. Read Ecclesiastes 2:17-19.[12] How did the writer (King Solomon) express his frustration with the results of his labors "under the sun"?

---

[10] **GENESIS 5**
29 He [Lamech] called his name Noah, saying, "This one shall give us rest from our work and from the toil of our hands arising from the ground which the LORD has cursed."

[11] **ROMANS 8**
19-22 The anxious longing of the creation waits eagerly for the revealing of the sons of God. For the creation was subjected to futility, not willingly, but because of Him who subjected it, in hope that the creation itself also will be set free from its slavery to corruption into the freedom of the glory of the children of God. For we know that the whole creation groans and suffers the pains of childbirth together until now.

[12] **ECCLESIASTES 2**
17-19 I hated life, for the work which had been done under the sun was grievous to me; because everything is futility and striving after wind. Thus I hated all the fruit of my labor . . . under the sun, for I must leave it to the man who will come after me. And who knows whether he will be a wise man or a fool?

[13] **2 PETER 3**
10 The day of the Lord will come like a thief, in which the heavens will pass away with a roar and the elements will be destroyed with intense heat, and the earth and its works will be burned up.

Solomon used the Hebrew word *hebel* to describe his work. *Hebel* is a primitive root word meaning "vapor, mere breath, empty, and delusionary."[T7]

Perhaps Solomon had noticed creation's entropy (the natural, continual degrading of all matter and energy in the universe). Everything on earth deteriorates, and we expend much energy just trying to slow the natural degradation. Yet we never make any real headway. True preservation is a delusion. To what, for example, will each of the following items eventually succumb?

cars:

houses:

grounds:

people:

Entropy affects everything. Whole careers, in fact, are maintenance-based. List some that come to mind.

From plastic surgeons to painters to pothole fillers, a surprising number of careers involve simply slowing the deterioration of people and things.

In addition to entropy, chaos rules in our corrupted world, both at home and at work.[T8] At home we can pick up our rooms or straighten our desks, but both will become disordered again with no real effort at all. At work we fight chaos in everything we do, from product design to production. Even people in creative jobs (commissioned artists or researchers) are not immune. And chaos especially reigns in human interactions. It takes a great deal of energy and effort to keep our relationships in order; just as it requires energy to prevent chaos in the world at large.

WORK IN A WAR ZONE

We mentioned earlier that sometimes our environment is resistant to the point of being hostile and frightening. List some elements of creation that pose danger and resist human efforts to manage or subdue them.

LANGUAGE & LIT:[T7]
MORE ON WORD STUDIES—In Bible study, we look up words in their languages of origin because it is helpful to glean the meanings from the culture in which the text was written. As we trace the definitions of the words (with their root words) and examine the tenses of the verbs, we are often enlightened and sometimes surprised.

The languages of origin for the Old Testament are Hebrew and Aramaic. The language of origin for the New Testament is Greek. None of these languages uses any form of the English alphabet. The only way to write them down, therefore, is to listen to the sound of the Hebrew or Greek word and then phonetically spell out those sounds with the English alphabet. This process is called transliteration.

There are a number of books, study Bibles, and computer programs that make word studies a simple process. One inexpensive tool is a concordance.

If you buy a concordance, be sure it corresponds to the version of the Bible you are using. Some of the most common translations are the *King James Version* (KJV), with several revised editions, the *New American Standard Bible* (NASB), and the *New International Version* (NIV). You will find a concordance available for each of these translations.

SCRIPTURE MEDITATION

Stand firm therefore, HAVING GIRDED YOUR LOINS WITH TRUTH, and HAVING PUT ON THE BREASTPLATE OF RIGHTEOUSNESS, and having shod YOUR FEET WITH THE PREPARATION OF THE GOSPEL OF PEACE; in addition to all, taking up the shield of faith with which you will be able to extinguish all the flaming arrows of the evil one. And take THE HELMET OF SALVATION, and the sword of the Spirit, which is the word of God. (Ephesians 6:14-17)

[14]**1 PETER 1**

17-19 If you address as Father the One who impartially judges according to each one's work, conduct yourselves in fear during the time of your stay on earth; knowing that you were not redeemed with perishable things like silver or gold from your futile way of life inherited from your forefathers, but with precious blood, as of a lamb unblemished and spotless, the blood of Christ.

23 For you have been born again not of seed which is perishable but imperishable, that is, through the living and enduring word of God.

[15]**DEUTERONOMY 7**

6-8 The LORD your God has chosen you to be a people for His own possession out of all the peoples who are on the face of the earth. The LORD did not set His love on you nor choose you because you were more in number than any of the peoples, for you were the fewest of all peoples, but because the LORD loved you and kept the oath which He swore to your forefathers, the LORD brought you out [of Egypt] by a mighty hand, and redeemed you from the house of slavery.

[16]**ROMANS 6 & 7**

6:17-18 Thanks be to God that though you were slaves of sin, you became obedient from the heart . . . , and having been freed from sin, you became slaves of righteousness.

7:14 We know that the Law is spiritual; but I am of flesh, sold into bondage to sin.

Dangers and problems abound in our natural world—weather conditions, earthquakes, floods, erosion, rough terrain, drought, insects, poisonous plants, dangerous animals, extremes in temperatures, deadly bacteria and diseases—the list goes on. Nevertheless, humankind has retained divinely appointed stewardship over God's created order, and our role in the earth's preservation and reproduction continues. Sin, however, has robbed each of us of the peace as well as the perpetual joy of *asah*—of making, producing, designing, and working as a subcreator in a cosmos that once welcomed us and yielded willingly to our control.

WHY BOTHER WITH WORK?

King Solomon wrestled with the sheer futility of working to acquire things that he couldn't take with him. Solomon also wrestled with the fact that he had no control over the one who would inherit the work of his hands. "What," Solomon asked in exasperation, "is the point?"

The apostle Peter takes this question to its ultimate conclusion. Read 2 Peter 3:10.[13] What will eventually happen to all of our achievements?

At the end of the ages, everything we've given our lives to develop, create, collect, invent, build, manage, or organize will be burned up. Not one of earth's treasures that we've craved or caressed will survive the consummation of the ages. Even our earth suits will be lost to the intense heat. But 1 Peter 1:17-19,23[14] offers hope. To whom?

According to 1 Peter 1:23,[14] what is the medium through which one becomes born again?

The Word of God, illuminated by the Holy Spirit, is a living and *enduring* message. It points to God's plan for "redeeming" us from this condemned cosmos through a process of rebirth. Redemption is an interesting concept. Read Deuteronomy 7:6-8.[15] From what were God's people redeemed?

In both Hebrew (*padah*) and Greek (*lutroo*), "to redeem" means "to gain release by paying a ransom." A ransom is the exchange price for something so valuable that the purchaser is willing to rescue, at any cost, what already belongs to him or her. Deuteronomy 7:6-8 speaks of God's redeeming (paying a ransom for) His own people to buy them back from slavery because He loved them and because He keeps His covenant promises.

God's people were in bondage in Egypt. Their physical bondage, however, was but a type or foreshadowing of what would one day be revealed about their spiritual condition in the preaching of the gospel.[T9] Read excerpts from Romans 6 and 7.[16] To what is everyone enslaved from birth?

Adam and Eve gave us quite an inheritance—a sin nature that enslaves us to Satan and condemns us to destruction! Our sin nature also put upon God the heavy onus of either leaving us to perish without hope or paying an unfathomable ransom price that we might be saved. Review 1 Peter 1:17-19,23.[14] With what ransom price were we made imperishable?

The apostle John tells us that God so loved the world that He gave His only begotten Son so that whoever believes in Him will not perish but will have eternal life (see John 3:16). Do you believe in Jesus and desire to obey God?

BRINGING IT HOME

1. Spend some time today thinking on the issue of your own slavery to sin and the price God paid to redeem or ransom you. Write God a thank-you note.

2. As you go about your work this week, pay attention to the things that go wrong. Note whether they went wrong from poor planning or from forces over which you had no control (such as weather, office politics, traffic jams, failed equipment, and so on). Pray before starting any new projects this week, asking God to minimize any impending chaos. Briefly note your progress on your daily calendar.

POINT OF INTEREST:[T8]

AN IRRESISTIBLE FORCE—
We've all experienced resistance when trying to do a simple household repair. More often than not, a small task will turn into a massive project. You'll find you have the wrong socket or you can't get the nail to go through. You'll begin to fix some surface problem, only to find that the whole foundation is rotten. We've learned by experience not to be too optimistic about the ease with which our work will be completed. In fact, the phenomenon that "anything that can go wrong, will" is so common that we've given it a name—Murphy's Law.

Paul tells in the book of Romans that creation itself is frustrated by its own corruption. Along with humankind, it is waiting to be redeemed. Someday this cosmos will be restored to a higher order. To get a glimpse of the new heaven and the new earth, read the last two chapters of Revelation. Compare what you read in Revelation with the first three chapters of Genesis. Both are listed in appendix A.

LANGUAGE & LIT:[T9]

OLD TESTAMENT SYMBOLISM—
We should read the Bible with this question in mind: *What does this say about redemption?* Old Testament characters and events were usually pictures that represented what would someday be a spiritual reality, namely, Jesus Christ and His redemptive work.

There is tremendous symbolism in the story of the Exodus. Egypt is a picture of bondage to sin, Moses is a picture (or type) of Christ the Redeemer, and the Promised Land is a picture of heaven. These life pictures "cast a forward shadow" of God's salvation plan.

[17]PSALM 90

16-17 Let Your work appear to Your servants, and Your majesty to their children. . . . And confirm for us the work of our hands; yes, confirm the work of our hands.

[18]JOB 1

10 Have You not made a hedge about him [Job] . . . , on every side? You have blessed the work of his hands, and his possessions have increased in the land.

[19]DEUTERONOMY 16

11-12,15 You shall rejoice before the LORD your God. . . . You shall remember that you were a slave in Egypt, and you shall be careful to observe these statutes. . . . Seven days you shall celebrate a feast to the LORD your God . . . , because the LORD your God will bless you in all your produce and in all the work of your hands, so that you will be altogether joyful.

[20]ECCLESIASTES 5

6 Do not let your speech cause you to sin. . . . Why should God be angry on account of your voice and destroy the work of your hands?

[21]HAGGAI 2

14,17 "So is this nation before Me," declares the LORD, "and . . . what they offer there is unclean. . . . [So] I smote you and every work of your hands with blasting wind, mildew and hail; yet you did not come back to Me," declares the LORD.

[22]DEUTERONOMY 28

11-13 (see page 00)

DAY 5

HOPE FOR REDEEMING OUR WORK

We learned on day 3 that God intended for our work to provide us with purpose and pleasure. On day 4, however, we saw that our work arena is a badly corrupted environment where entropy, chaos, and sin reign. Moreover, our world is destined to total destruction; ultimately, our works will be exposed to its consuming fire. Do these truths affect your motivation to work? If so, how?

The temporal nature of our efforts is bothersome to many of us, for preserving "things" is a way of leaving a legacy or a marker of our own existence. The ancients built castles, great walls, and pyramids as lasting memorials to themselves. Today we build bridges and buildings for much the same reason. The desire to create with purpose and permanence is inherent in our human nature.[T10] It even shows up in Scripture. Read Psalm 90:16-17.[17] What does the psalmist ask of God? *Confirm the work of our hands.*

In the midst of a cursed environment, the psalmist is asking God to give the people lasting fruit for their labors. Because God Himself cursed the earth, is this prayer consistent with His intentions? What insights do you see from Job 1:10[18] and Deuteronomy 16:11-12,15?[18]

Because of its corruption, our world will always frustrate our work efforts to the point that neither our work nor our workplace will run smoothly for very long. On the other hand, God still desires for our work to be not only a source of material and financial rewards (temporal value), but also a purposeful and deeply satisfying source of joy! Work concerns not only the product of our labor (this should be done with excellence as unto the Lord), but also the process of our labor (the focus of our hearts).

These parallel realities explain the dual nature of work and help us understand why we have such a love-hate relationship with it. Work is, and will always be, a source of both pleasure and pain. We must learn to live with the tension between these two extremes. If you could divide into percentages the pleasure and pain of your average workday (for a total of 100 percent), how would the numbers come out?

Pain: _____ Neutral: _____ Pleasure: _____

Hopefully, your neutral plus pleasure percentages outscore your percent of frustration or pain. If your pain level is higher, you may be in the wrong job or field, may be working with difficult people, or may simply be in a trial of your faith. It's possible, however, that the cause of your frustration and dissatisfaction from work comes from having goals that are not aligned with God's plans and purposes. Compare Job 1:10[18] and Deuteronomy 16:11-12,15[19] with Ecclesiastes 5:6[20] and Haggai 2:14,17.[21]

From the verses in Ecclesiastes and Haggai, what would you say was keeping God from blessing the people's work efforts? *Speech of sin and turning away from God.*

According to Deuteronomy 28:11-13,[22] what releases God to bless human labor? *Gods promise to our Forefathers.*

Whether it's a nail we can't hammer into place or a proposal that fails to secure a contract, few things rankle us like failing to reap the fruit of our labors. Yet, according to these verses, God Himself intentionally frustrates our efforts at times. He will probe this "tender spot" to bring us to obedience or to turn our attention toward working for things that matter.

What "Things" Matter to God?

How do we know what matters to God? Go back and review 2 Peter 3:10[13] from yesterday's study. What is destined for destruction, and whose created works are thereby affected? *heaven and earth and all of our works*

What, then, is the eternal value of the cosmos? *?*

If much of God's own works are destined for destruction, how much more the works of our hands! And God intends to rescue very little from the ultimate demise of His

POINT OF INTEREST:[T10]
TEMPORAL VALUE VERSUS ETERNAL VALUE—While the products of our hands have no eternal value, they may have temporal value, especially as we create or operate in ways that improve the quality of life for others. But even altruistic work cannot by itself satisfy our longing for purpose and meaning, nor can it provide us with an inner sense of achievement.

After fifty-seven years of political work in England, Leonard Wolfe, a well-known author, said, "Meditating on the history of Britain and the world since 1914, I see clearly that I achieved practically nothing. I have, therefore, to make the rather ignominious confession to myself and to anyone who may read this book that I must have in a long life ground through between 150,000 and 200,000 hours of perfectly useless work."

If we're honest, most of us have to admit that, even when our work is extraordinarily complex, it amounts (in the larger scheme of things) to little more than a steady stream of relatively meaningless activities. The significance and sense of purpose we so deeply long for in our work will never be found, except in its connection to the purposes of God. Ironically, we fulfill His purposes by living out the Christian life in the workplace, where we do our best to produce something of temporal value with our hands.

Scripture Meditation
If we say that we have no sin, we are deceiving ourselves, and the truth is not in us. If we confess our sins, He is faithful and righteous to forgive us our sins and to cleanse us from all unrighteousness.
(1 John 1:8-9)

²³**MATTHEW 24**

35 "Heaven and earth will pass away, but My words shall not pass away."

²⁴**JOHN 5**

17,19-20 [Jesus] answered them, "My Father is working until now, and I Myself am working. . . . Truly, truly, I say to you, . . . whatever the Father does, these things the Son also does in like manner. For the Father loves the Son, and shows Him all things that He Himself is doing."

²⁵**JOHN 6**

27-29 [Jesus said,] "Do not work for the food which perishes, but for the food which endures to eternal life, which the Son of Man shall give to you. . . ." Therefore they said to Him, "What shall we do, so that we may work the works of God?" Jesus answered . . . , "This is the work of God, that you believe in Him whom He has sent."

²⁶**JOHN 4**

34 Jesus said to them, "My food is to do the will of Him who sent Me and to accomplish His work."

²⁷**1 CORINTHIANS 3**

11-15 No man can lay a foundation other than the one which is laid, which is Jesus Christ. Now if any man builds on the foundation with gold, silver, precious stones, wood, hay, straw, each man's work will become evident; for the day will show it, because it is to be revealed with fire; and the fire itself will test the quality of each man's work. If any man's work which he has built on it remains, he shall receive a reward. If any man's work is burned up, he will suffer loss; but he himself will be saved, yet so as through fire.

own created order—actually, only two things will be made imperishable. These treasures are mentioned in Matthew 24:35[23] and 1 Peter 1:17-19,23.[14] What are they?

God's Word   The blood of Christ

As we learned in day 4, the Father values us beyond our understanding, and He provided for us a way of redemption, paying as the ransom price the blood of His own Son. He also values His Word and will redeem it in the day of destruction. If our work efforts are to have any redeeming value, then they must contribute in some way to God's agenda, that is, to preserving the things that He values.[T11]

THE WORKING MODEL

We come to understand God's agenda through His Word. Read John 5:17,19-20[24] and list the workers.

How does the Son know what to do?

By watching the Father

Note the present tense—the Father and the Son *are* working and have been working right up through the present moment. As Jesus looked to God the Father for training and instruction, so also must we look to Jesus as our role model for doing the works (*ergon*) of God. Read John 6:27-29.[25] What is the basic and essential work of God, and for what should we work?

Believing in him whom God sent.

The Father instructs us to believe in the Son, and the Son instructs us to work for "food" that endures. Read John 4:34.[26] How does Jesus define that "food"? *"My food is*

To do the will of him who sent me.

Let's add one more Scripture before we conclude this day's study. Compare 2 Peter 3:10[13] and 1 Corinthians 3:11-15.[27] What do these Scriptures have in common?

Fire will come and destroy man's work

According to 1 Corinthians 3:11-15, what works will pass the fire test? On what must they be built?

only s. Built on God.

The apostle Paul (the writer of the letters to the Corinthians) compares the works of things that will easily burn and are of little value to things that are imperishable and priceless.

All of our works will indeed be tried by fire. Those works that have only temporal value will be destroyed. But those works that have been built on the foundation that Jesus Christ has already laid will go with us into eternity because they have contributed to the kingdom of our Lord.

Our goal over the remainder of this course is to look at the ways we can approach our work with purpose so that we might produce those priceless things that will remain.

BRINGING IT HOME

1. Jesus said, "Truly, truly, I say to you, he who hears My word, and believes Him who sent Me, has eternal life, and does not come into judgment, but has passed out of death into life" (John 5:24). Does the way you live your life and approach your work reflect that you (1) believe in God's promise of eternal life and (2) are confident that you will be rewarded for works that achieve His goals? If so, thank God for His master plan and ask Him to increase your awareness of His goals as you go about your workday. If not, do you really believe in the One whom God has sent? Write down your thoughts.

2. Look at the percentage points you gave to pain on page 25. Write down three changes that you think would reduce the frustration of your work situation. If any of these are changes within your control, implement one of them this week. If they are not, ask God to either remove the stress area or to show you how to deal more effectively with the painful situation(s).

POINT OF INTEREST:[T11]

THE WORTH OF WORK—If we stopped to evaluate work from an eternal perspective, we'd see how absolutely upside-down our value system really is. If asked who is most productive, we'd probably look to the man who has spent his life neglecting his family, steam-rolling relationships, using people to get ahead, and gaining position, power, and a large bucket of "mammon," all of which is destined to perish. At the same time, we would overlook the woman who decided to work at home and care for her children. In fact, such women are sometimes looked down upon. Yet mothers play a tremendous role in shaping young lives, who not only will contribute to society someday but will also live eternally!

We have a skewed mentality. There's nothing unbiblical about a woman working outside the home. But the point is, our culture demeans an extremely important job: raising children in the discipline and admonition of the Lord. We must recognize that this effort is primary for the health and well-being of our society as well as for the advancing of the kingdom of God.

We need to reexamine our yardsticks and value those who cultivate people rather than those who accumulate wealth, power, and position.

SCRIPTURE MEDITATION

Stand firm therefore, having girded your loins with truth, and having put on the breastplate of righteousness, and having shod your feet with the preparation of the gospel of peace; in addition to all, taking up the shield of faith with which you will be able to extinguish all the flaming missiles of the evil one. And take the helmet of salvation, and the sword of the Spirit, which is the word of God. (Ephesians 6:14-17)

To the leader: You will need a flipchart or other large sheet of paper for the Hebrew and Greek word definitions in the first two activities.

1. The English language uses a variety of words to describe work, and these words give us some insight into our society's attitudes toward work. However, if we want to get God's perspective on work, we have to look at biblical terms for it.

   • Complete this sentence: "When I think about my work, I feel . . . "

   • Using a flipchart or other large sheet of paper, write your own definitions for the Hebrew words *abodah* and *amal*.

2. In addition to *abodah* and *amal*, a couple of other words in biblical Hebrew describe work. Likewise, New Testament Greek provides a pair of relevant terms for our study.

   • Complete the list of definitions started in activity 1 by writing your own definitions of *asah, maaseh, kopiao,* and *ergon*. (You may wish to keep this list of words around for reference throughout your study of work.)

   • Which of the definitions on the list comes closest to describing your own experiences with work? Why?

3. God is the Creator, and that means He is a worker. Furthermore, even before the Fall, God gave work assignments to Adam and Eve as a way to meet the human need for purpose and creative expression. Our first ancestors' experience of work was productive and joyful.

   • What words or phrases would you use to describe God's work in creating and sustaining the universe?

   • Pretend that you are Adam or Eve and that you have just come home in the evening. Your spouse says, "Hi, honey. How was your day?" Describe what your workday was like. (If you're a bit of a ham, you might even want to pair up with another member of the group and do this as an improvisational skit.)

   • What evidences do you see that work today still fulfills the human need for purpose and creative expression?

4. After their sin, Adam and Eve's relationship to work changed dramatically—and for the worse. Since then, the situation hasn't changed much. We retain the role of stewards over God's created order, but our work is plagued by difficulty, frustration, and even futility. All this reminds us that we need a Savior.

   • What are some of the negative aspects of work as we experience it today? What's the connection between these things and sin?

   • Do you ever get the sense that the services you provide or the goods you produce in your work are ultimately meaningless? If so, why?

   • Take a few moments to write a prayer expressing to God how you feel about the redemption of sinners through the blood of Jesus. (Note: If you haven't yet been redeemed, or if you aren't sure about it, please speak with a spiritually mature Christian about your need.)

5. Despite the effects of sin, God still wants our work to meet our material needs and to give us pleasure. What He's concerned about most, however, is *how* we do our work, not *what* we do, for if we do our work in a way that's consistent with eternal values, it will not go to waste.

   • Would you say that you have a love-hate relationship with your work? Why?

   • Is your work aligned with the purposes of God? Explain why you think it is or is not.

   • Do you believe there was a time in your life when God intentionally frustrated your work efforts in order to get your attention and pull you back on track? If so, tell about it.

   • How can your work contribute to the building up of the kingdom of God?

Close the group time with a prayer asking God to help each member of the group do his or her work in a way that contributes to the building up of His kingdom. Thank Him for the redemption He provided at the cost of His Son's life so that we would not have to lead lives that end up being consumed in fire.

INTRODUCTION TO UNIT 2
CHOOSING OUR WORK

Destination: To examine the biblical process of making career choices.

A boy ran into the local drug store and asked the pharmacist to use the phone. Quickly he dialed the number of a nearby grocer. "I heard you were looking for a delivery boy and I want to apply for the job," he said breathlessly. When the grocer told him he had already hired someone, the boy asked, "Well, what if he doesn't work out? Could I call you later to see if he's still around?"

"I think he'll work out fine," the grocer answered. "I'm quite pleased with his work so far."

When the boy hung up, the pharmacist said, "Don't worry, son. With an attitude like that, you'll find a job in no time!"

"I already have a job," the young man replied. "I'm the grocer's delivery boy. I just wanted to see how I was doing."

Wouldn't it be nice if it were that easy to select a career and find out how you're doing? It isn't! Many do a poor job of choosing their vocation and then find themselves in fields for which they are ill suited. Once they've invested in an education or started a family or established a certain spending level, however, they feel trapped in jobs they don't really like. Others may have planned well, only to find that their jobs are becoming either more and more narrow or forever altered by advancing technologies.

Downsizing corporations and evolving job descriptions will probably remain the norm. Career analysts are currently projecting, in fact, that today's college graduates will have a number of different careers (not just jobs) before they retire. Even those who are past the midpoint of their work lives will probably be affected by changes in the workplace or even by their own desire to change career direction.

Proverbs 19:21 tells us, "Many plans are in a man's heart, but the counsel of the LORD will stand," while Proverbs 16:9 says, "The mind of man plans his way, but the LORD directs his steps." Whether preparing for a career or preparing for a career change, we need to know how to proceed God's way. In unit 2 we will examine the biblical approach to selecting and sustaining a career.

DAY 1

IS WORK OPTIONAL?

[28]**PROVERBS 12**
24 The hand of the diligent will rule, but the slack hand will be put to forced labor.

[29]**DEUTERONOMY 15**
10-11 You shall generously give to [the poor], and your heart shall not be grieved when you give. . . . For the poor will never cease to be in the land; therefore I command you, saying, "You shall freely open your hand to . . . your needy and poor in your land."

[30]**2 THESSALONIANS 3**
10-12 For even when we were with you, we used to give you this order: if anyone is not willing to work, then he is not to eat, either. For we hear that some among you are leading an undisciplined life, doing no work at all, but acting like busybodies. Now such persons we command and exhort in the Lord Jesus Christ to work in quiet fashion and eat their own bread.

[31]**PROVERBS 16**
26 A worker's appetite works for him, for his hunger urges him on.

[32]**1 TIMOTHY 5**
8 But if any one does not provide for his own, and especially for those of his household, he has denied the faith and is worse than an unbeliever.

[33]**DEUTERONOMY 5**
12-14 Observe the sabbath day to keep it holy, as the LORD your God commanded you. Six days you shall labor and do all your work, but the seventh day is a sabbath of the LORD your God; in it you shall not do any work.

In unit 1 we rated our jobs on an Employment Enjoyment Scale. Check your job score (page 12) and write it below.

Even if you like your job, it's unlikely that you gave it a perfect score. Few people would. Whether your job is ideal or you prefer to not work at all, God has seen to it that there are both external and internal motivators for prodding us (and every other human being) to work. What work incentives do you see from Proverbs 12:24?[28]

Americans are unfamiliar with slavery. Still, most of us began our work lives at a fairly young age, with increasingly complex chores imposed on us by our parents. Anyone who hasn't learned to work by adulthood will experience the negative force of social rejection, for in every society all able-bodied persons are expected to support themselves. Compare Deuteronomy 15:10-11[29] and 2 Thessalonians 3:10-12.[30] Is society's attitude biblical or unbiblical? Is it appropriate or too harsh? Support your answer.

What should happen to people who won't work, according to 2 Thessalonians 3:10-12?

Christians must give to those who *cannot* work, that is, those who are helplessly needy. But supporting those who simply *will not* work is unbiblical. Work is foundational to personal and societal survival—so much so that in some societies labor is forced by the threat of violence or physical harm.

Read Proverbs 16:26.[31] What internal force motivates us to work, according to this proverb?

If external forces didn't impose work on us, internal forces would. Our appetites—both physical hunger and material needs and desires—are strong and highly motivating drivers. Except for a privileged few, work is inescapable. It is vital to human existence and survival.

Providing for ourselves through work is also a scriptural mandate. Read 1 Timothy 5:8.[32] What do you learn from this passage concerning your work responsibilities?

Far more damaging than society's disapproval are the consequences of disobedience to God's Word. God calls laziness "sin." Refusing to work, then, can have eternal, as well as temporal, consequences.

One of the Ten Commandments deals with the issue of work. Read Deuteronomy 5:12-14.[33] What work instructions do these verses offer us?

Laziness may be a growing problem in our society, but presently it is far less prevalent than our tendency to overwork. We are a nation of excesses, and workaholism is an ever-present temptation. For this reason, we lean toward only partial recall of the work commandment. That is, we focus on observing the Sabbath day and keeping it holy because that's the part most of us have trouble with. It's our cultural norm to work hard during the work week and even harder doing our weekend chores. It is *not* our cultural norm to rest on the Sabbath.

What do you think people are trying to achieve by overworking? That is, what motivates workaholics?[T12]

Another significant internal motivator for working is the desire for success. In the eyes of the world, success is the

POINT OF INTEREST:[T12]

WORKAHOLISM—If our jobs demand so much of our time and energy that we don't have time to cultivate our deepest relationships with God, our families, and others, then we're simply working too much. There comes a point where you have to consider why you work so much and what your own personal convictions must be concerning how much you will work.

Most people say they overwork because they need the extra money (or that if they don't, they'll lose income). But few have ever asked themselves, *How much money is enough?* Ask yourself this question and then live by it. Also ask, *If this is enough for my present time and I were to attain more, what would I do with the rest?*

If we don't establish a limit for consuming our own wealth, then the amount that is enough will always be a moving target. We'll respond like John D. Rockefeller when asked, "How much is enough?" He answered, "Another dollar more." If that is your attitude as well, you will never be content with your income.

A few people have established a point of personal consumption that is enough; they give the rest to be used in God's kingdom or in a charity as unto the Lord. These people are rare, but you could be one of them. There will be a day when we will have to give an account of how we used the resources God gave us to expand His kingdom. God's mill grinds slowly, but it grinds exceedingly fine. Those who honor Him, He will honor.

[34] ECCLESIASTES 5

10 He who loves money will not be satisfied with money, nor he who loves abundance with its income. This too is vanity.

[35] DEUTERONOMY 8

6-7,9 You shall keep the commandments of the LORD your God, to walk in His ways and to fear Him. For the LORD your God is bringing you into a good land . . . where you will eat food without scarcity, in which you will not lack anything.

10-14,17-18 When you have eaten and are satisfied, you shall bless the LORD your God for the good land which He has given you. Beware that you don't forget the LORD your God by not keeping His commandments and His ordinances and His statutes which I am commanding you today; otherwise, when you have eaten and are satisfied, and have built good houses and lived in them, . . . and all that you have multiplies, then your heart will become proud and you will forget the LORD your God who brought you out from the land of Egypt, out of the house of slavery. . . . Otherwise, you may say in your heart, "My power and the strength of my hand made me this wealth." But you shall remember the LORD your God, for it is He who is giving you power to make wealth, that He may confirm His covenant which He swore to your fathers, as it is this day.

gold standard; money and power are the measures of having "arrived" or having "made one's mark" in the world. In search of success, many people in our culture go from one ambitious project (or deal or scheme) to the next. They plan to slow down as soon as they get this company started or get that promotion. These men and women are setting themselves up for disappointment.

Read Ecclesiastes 5:10.[34] What "vanity" is expressed in this verses?

Most of us know (at least on one level) that "things" do not satisfy. Those objects we have our hearts set on never really fulfill our longing, and rarely are we even surprised! The joy in "things" will always be fleeting, for our hearts hunger for more than this world can afford. Instead of grasping this truth, however, we tend to look for the next "fix," as if we really believe the next accomplishment or acquisition will be the ticket to contentment.[T13]

Being even temporarily satisfied with material possessions or earthly successes, however, is problematic. Read Deuteronomy 8:6-7,9,10-14,17-18.[35] What temptation follows wealth and success?

Feeling satisfied with our accomplishments or attainments tempts us into thinking that our success is self-made. We forget the Source of our supply, or we take more credit for our successes than is our due. We forget about God, and we fail to thank Him and give Him praise. But our human accomplishments are of no value to God. He is not interested in what we have made, nor in the amount of wealth we've attained, nor in the degree of power in our position.

God is vitally interested, however, in the *process* of our work, that is, in the spiritual maturity we gain *through* our work and the things we accomplish *within* our work arena that build up the kingdom of God.

BRINGING IT HOME

1. When our work is done to serve God or to please God, then our efforts assume an eternal quality; it's a process that endures, even when the work itself is finished. How would embracing this truth change your workday?

2. Consider the spiritual needs of your coworkers. As God's ambassador, do you exhibit Christlike qualities that create an appetite in your coworkers for the things of God? Think of at least one thing you could be doing differently to be a better ambassador for Christ; then implement that change into your next workday.

POINT OF INTEREST:[T13]

CONSUMING WEALTH—
Sometimes people aren't as concerned with accumulating wealth as they are with spending it. King Solomon had a problem many of us wish we had, namely, having more abundance than he could consume. It led him to excesses that brought down his kingdom. Read the following passage from Ecclesiastes 2:4-11.

"I enlarged my works: I built houses for myself, I planted vineyards for myself; I made gardens and parks for myself and I planted in them all kinds of fruit trees. . . . I possessed flocks and herds larger than all who preceded me in Jerusalem. Also, I collected for myself silver and gold, and the treasure of kings and provinces. . . . All that my eyes desired I did not refuse them. I did not withhold my heart from any pleasure, for my heart was pleased because of all my labor and this was my reward for all my labor. Thus I considered all my activities which my hands had done and the labor which I had exerted, and behold all was vanity and striving after wind and there was no profit under the sun."

God sometimes allows us enough rope to hang ourselves with. Our earthly desires are then choked out by the very abundance of things we've accumulated in our greed. We collect much and we care for none of it. Things become burdensome. Often, the one with nothing else to desire is far worse off than the one who has little but his or her dreams, because our doctored illusions are free of the weight and the worry of dreams realized.

SCRIPTURE MEDITATION

By wisdom a house is built, and by understanding it is established; and by knowledge the rooms are filled with all precious and pleasant riches. (Proverbs 24:3-4)

DAY 2

CAREER: CHOICE OR CALLING?

There's little difference between the way Christians and non-Christians select their careers. Both look for a vocation that provides the optimal combination of personal interest, required training, and good pay. How did you come to your career decision? Did God call you into your vocation, did you choose a career path, or did you just fall into whatever became available?[T14]

Personal interest, training opportunities, and compensation are all legitimate considerations. But how do they fit with biblical models? Let's examine the careers of some Bible heroes by reading 1 Samuel 16:1,13[36] and Jeremiah 1:4-7.[37] Fill in the chart below:

Hero	Called To	At Age

The Scriptures are filled with accounts of people who were called directly into an area of work—Noah, Joseph, Samson, and Gideon (to name a few). From the Scripture references above, we see that God called David, a shepherd boy, to be king over Israel, and Jeremiah, a youth, to be a prophet to the nations.

Do you think God calls people into positions today? If so, into what kinds of careers?

If you are like most people, you might be thinking, *God calls people into missions or ministries, but He doesn't call us into our secular work.* Consider Exodus 31:1,3,6,[38] 1 Kings 7:13-14,[39] and 2 Chronicles 2:13-14.[40] How were the artisans and craftsmen trained for their various trades? Circle all that may apply:

personal aptitude   apprenticeships
Holy Spirit   trade school
on-the-job training

Sidebar references

[36]**1 SAMUEL 16**
1,13 The LORD said to Samuel . . . "Fill your horn with oil and go; I will send you to Jesse the Bethlehemite, for I have selected a king for Myself among his sons." . . . Then Samuel took the horn of oil and anointed [David]; . . . and the Spirit of the LORD came mightily upon David from that day forward.

[37]**JEREMIAH 1**
4-7 The word of the Lord came to me [Jeremiah] saying, . . . "I have appointed you a prophet to the nations." Then I said, "Alas, Lord God! Behold, I do not know how to speak, because I am a youth." But the LORD said to me, "Do not say, 'I am a youth,' . . . and all that I command you, you shall speak."

[38]**EXODUS 31**
1,3,6 The Lord spoke to Moses, saying, "See, I have called by name Bezalel. . . . I have filled him with the Spirit of God in wisdom, in understanding, in knowledge, and in all kinds of craftsmanship. . . . And in the hearts of all who are skillful I have put skill, that they may make all that I have commanded you."

[39]**1 KINGS 7**
13-14 King Solomon sent and brought Hiram from Tyre . . . , a worker in bronze; and he was filled with wisdom and understanding and skill for doing any work in bronze.

[40]**2 CHRONICLES 2**
13-14 Now I am sending Huram-abi, a skilled man, endowed with understanding, . . . who knows how to work in gold, silver, bronze, iron, stone and wood, and in purple, violet, linen and crimson fabrics.

God certainly may have used any or all of the above to give these workers their remarkable skills. But Exodus 31 tells us specifically that God, through the Spirit, filled Bezalel with wisdom, understanding, knowledge, and craftsmanship. "Filled" in the Hebrew is *mala* (or *male*). It means "to be full to overflowing, complete, drenched."

Other Scriptures indicate that the abilities of these men seemed inherent; that is, they were each endowed with wisdom and skill in a particular area. "Endowed" (*yada*) means "intimate knowledge; certainty." The word carries the idea of natural ability being honed into a high level of skill that enabled them to produce and create with superior quality.

Consider your own natural abilities and interests. Write down two or three areas where you seem to have a natural bent. Think back to when you first recognized this skill or area of interest. What life stage were you in?

<u>Natural Abilities</u>   <u>Life Stage</u>

Perhaps you are in a job that does not use your natural talents or interests. Or perhaps your interests have changed in midcareer or you've discovered a new skill or talent that has been lying dormant. Is it too late to change jobs? Read the Scriptures in appendix A for unit 2. Fill in the chart below:

<u>Men Called</u>   <u>To Do What?</u>

Peter

Andrew

Paul

Abraham

Moses

Peter, Andrew, and Paul were called in midcareer. Both Abraham and Moses were called at an age when most of us are ready to retire. Even when we allow for their greater life span, they illustrate ongoing endeavor until the end of

POINT OF INTEREST:[T14]
SEEKING GOD'S WILL—We can easily get bogged down seeking God's will for our careers. In fact, sometimes we become downright immobilized.

Insight into God's will for our lives comes as we obey what we already know to be true. The further along we go in our walk with God and the more we seek His counsel in Scripture, the more insight God will provide. We already know, for example, that it is God's will for us to put Christ first in every area of our lives. We know it is His will that we love and serve others. We know that it is God's will for us to share the gospel and to make disciples in whatever circle of influence we have been given. And we know it is God's will for us to look to Him as the One who will ultimately meet our needs.

When we start moving forward in the things we already know, we will automatically be headed in the right direction. We become more keenly aware of God's presence and more able to recognize His voice. Building on the value of these experiences, we begin to learn to tell the difference between when we are operating in our own strength and when we are leaning on His all-sufficiency.

As we walk in the light of what we know, our experience of God will increase and our awareness of His presence will become clear. We still won't be able to define these experiences any more than we can define time and space. Nevertheless, as we move forward and trust God, we will come to rest securely in His approval and in the knowledge that we are operating in the very center of His will in every area of our lives.

[41]**PSALM 139**

13-16 For You formed my inward parts; You wove me in my mother's womb. I will give thanks to You, for I am fearfully and wonderfully made; wonderful are Your works, and my soul knows it very well. My frame was not hidden from You, when I was made in secret, and skillfully wrought in the depths of the earth. Your eyes have seen my unformed substance; and in Your book were all written, the days that were ordained for me, when as yet there was not one of them.

[42]**JEREMIAH 1**

4-5 Now the word of the LORD came to me saying, "Before I formed you in the womb I knew you, and before you were born I consecrated you; I have appointed you a prophet to the nations."

their journeys. Briefly look over the Scripture references in the Road Map column on page 34 for insights on how each man was called. In the list below, check all that apply to their calling:

___ They were called directly.
___ They were called by God Himself.
___ They were called by name.
___ They were called for a specific purpose.
___ They were called in God's timing.
___ They were called at their convenience.
___ They understood their call.
___ They were called by a spiritual leader.

Whether into ministry or into craftsmanship, God Himself called each man individually *by name,* and He called them into a specific work. Moreover, each of these men recognized his calling. They not only knew what they were called to do, but also knew precisely how to do it. Do you believe God has called you or is able to call you into a specific work? Why or why not?

Read Psalm 139:13-16[41] and Jeremiah 1:4-5.[42] When were these writers given their calling?

The world would have us believe that we can choose whatever career path we want.[T15] But wisdom tells us we each have a focus or direction—a calling that draws and guides us through the process of life. God designs us in our mother's womb and weaves into our being all the necessary ingredients we will need to follow our calling. He then allows things like family and circumstances to mold and shape us around those innate talents. He also arranges opportunities for us to hone our skills until we are filled to overflowing with the knowledge and ability to perform our assigned tasks.

This doesn't mean that some will not be more gifted or more talented than others. But it does mean that God, through His Spirit, will equip us to perform at whatever level of expertise His assignment requires. Our training experiences may not be easy, but God will take our pain and use it for our good and for His glory as we yield to His call on our lives.

BRINGING IT HOME

1. In this study session you listed some skills and attributes that seemed to be innate. Consider the extent to which you use these skills in your primary job. If you use your natural skills highly in your vocation, thank God for guiding you into a suitable career. Ask Him to help you make full use of the skills He has given to you so that you might be an exemplary Christian employee.

2. If your innate skills are not used in your current job, consider what kinds of jobs would make use of your innate talents. List these jobs below and place a check beside positions that might be offered at your current workplace.

3. Do any of the jobs you've listed above have more appeal to you than does your current job? If so, begin seeking God's will about making a career change. Even if you anticipate eventually changing your place of employment, ask God to open doors for you now to begin honing your talents and skills in your current workplace.

POINT OF INTEREST:[T15]

REFRAMING OUR MIND-SET—To understand the difference between the Ptolemaic view of a geocentric solar system (where the planets revolve around the earth) versus the Copernican view of a heliocentric solar system (where the planets revolve around the sun), we have to make a shift in the way we view things—looking at the planets and interpreting the data in a totally different way.

To understand the difference between the world's system and kingdom principles, we must make a similar shift in the way we view life and interpret the data. Even in the workplace, kingdom principles will be predominantly counter-cultural. So when presented with those principles, new believers often respond, "How can we do those things in the *real* world?"

The answer is "God's kingdom *is* the real world." This doesn't mean that the earth is not real, but that the earth is temporal while God's kingdom is eternal, and the earth is still subject to the sovereign Lord. To focus on the temporal, therefore, is to have our perspective out of whack, for we can't define the permanent by the transient.

This means that we must accept divine wisdom over earthly wisdom and embrace divine truths even when they fly in the face of conventional wisdom. We must not slack off at work, but we must grasp the urgency of the here and now, trying for all we're worth to complete the "real" work God has given us to do. Our workplace is a daily appointment where we, as God's ambassadors, can reflect kingdom principles and values.

SCRIPTURE MEDITATION

THINGS WHICH EYE HAS NOT SEEN AND EAR HAS NOT HEARD, AND WHICH HAVE NOT ENTERED THE HEART OF MAN, ALL THAT GOD HAS PREPARED FOR THOSE WHO LOVE HIM.
(1 Corinthians 2:9)

DAY 3

CAREER: SECULAR OR SPIRITUAL?

Most of us make a clear distinction between secular work and ministry. But is that a biblical concept for believers? Read Revelation 1:5-6[43] and 1 Peter 2:9.[44] What is the primary job title for every person who has been released from sin and called out of darkness to serve in the kingdom of God?

God established and ordained a priesthood in Israel that served as a type or foreshadow of the priesthood of Jesus. Read 1 Peter 2:9[44] again as well as Mark 16:15[45] and Matthew 28:19-20.[46] What priestly duties are assigned to the disciples of God, according to these passages?

-

-

-

If you name the name of Christ and have been set at liberty through His blood, you *are* in full-time ministry. No matter where your sphere of service is, you are still a *royal priest* unto God. Therefore, your career is not an end in itself but a vehicle and a context for your ministry—a place in which you are called to be salt and light, a sphere in which you love and serve people with the love of Christ.

This does not sound like an easy assignment for those employed outside the religious community. How can one proclaim the excellencies of God, preach the gospel, make disciples, and teach God's commandments when he or she is being paid to organize, design, manage, develop, or produce?

Read 1 Corinthians 10:31-33,[47] Ephesians 6:5,7,[48] and 2 Thessalonians 3:7-9.[49] What insights do these Scriptures give you concerning the work responsibilities of a Christian?

In their zeal to spread the gospel, some people wrongly use their work hours for preaching instead of producing.

---

[43]**REVELATION 1**
5,6 From Jesus Christ, the faithful witness, the firstborn of the dead, and the ruler of the kings of the earth. To Him who loves us and released us from our sins by His blood—and He has made us to be a kingdom, priests to His God and Father—to Him be the glory and the dominion forever and ever. Amen.

[44]**1 PETER 2**
9 You are A CHOSEN RACE, A ROYAL PRIESTHOOD, A HOLY NATION, A PEOPLE FOR God's OWN POSSESSION, so that you may proclaim the excellencies of Him who has called you out of darkness into His marvelous light.

[45]**MARK 16**
15 [Jesus] said to [His disciples], "Go into all the world and preach the gospel to all creation."

[46]**MATTHEW 28**
19-20 "Go therefore and make disciples of all the nations, baptizing them in the name of the Father and the Son and the Holy Spirit, teaching them to observe all that I commanded you."

[47]**1 CORINTHIANS 10**
31-33 Whether . . . you eat or drink or whatever you do, do all to the glory of God. Give no offense . . . ; please all men in all things.

[48]**EPHESIANS 6**
5,7 Slaves, be obedient to those who are your masters according to the flesh, with fear and trembling, in the sincerity of your heart. . . . With good will render service, as to the Lord.

[49]**THESSALONIANS 3**
7-9 (see page 141)

38

Our call, however, is to be exemplary workers, whether we are in a secular or a religious environment. We lift up Christ by our productivity, our quality, our attitude, our refusal to gossip, our gentle spirit, our kind treatment of others, and so on. When the opportunity comes to share the good news, an exemplary worker will be able to do so without cheating his or her employer out of labor hours.[T16]

Bearing in mind the previous Scriptures and insights, summarize the difference between a "secular" job and a "spiritual" job.

We've said that all Christians are called to full-time ministry, but that doesn't mean that all Christians are fulfilling their duty. One individual works in a factory and has a heart focused on serving Christ. Another individual works in a religious arena, but his heart focus is on advancing his career. Which one is serving as a priest in the workplace? Why?

The world—and the church—categorically define Christian service and secular work by environment. But God defines it by the focus of our hearts. This means that one can be working in the church, in missions, or in a parachurch ministry and still have a secular job because his or her heart is focused on worldly success rather than on the things of God.

Read 1 Corinthians 10:31-33[47] again. How are we to do all our work?

We cannot compartmentalize our lives. We can't chase a buck from nine to five and then go "do our ministry." A biblical vision sees every component of our lives under the lordship of Christ. We have integrity only insofar as we are the same kind of person with the same godly pursuits, no matter where we are placed in service.

PURPOSE AND MEANING

As we learned in yesterday's study, God had a plan for each of us before we were ever conceived. That plan is in no way marred by circumstances of our birth, upbringing, or any other conditions over which we've had no control.

HISTORY & CULTURE:[T16]

WORKING AS UNTO THE LORD—I (Ken) was in England in 1984 when a number of statues in the sanctuary of the Westminster Cathedral were, for the first time, removed for cleaning. To everyone's amazement, they discovered that the work on the back of the statues (which is never seen) was just as good as the work on the front. Apparently, the artists had done their work to the best of their creative ability and for an audience of one: God.

Work, especially today, does not always afford us the time to do our best. Nevertheless, there ought to be a quality in our work as if it were all done for the audience of one. People have a right to expect the highest standards and the most careful efforts from Christians because we understand that our audience is impartial and His standards are absolute.

SCRIPTURE MEDITATION

You also, as living stones, are being built up as a spiritual house for a holy priesthood, to offer up spiritual sacrifices acceptable to God through Jesus Christ. (1 Peter 2:5)

⁵⁰ACTS 7

21-24,26,28-30 Pharaoh's daughter [found Moses in a basket and she raised him] as her own son. Moses was educated in all the learning of the Egyptians, and he was a man of power in words and deeds. . . . [Nearing] the age of forty, . . . he saw one of [his brethren] being treated unjustly [by an Egyptian, and Moses killed him]. . . . On the following day [a Hebrew slave said,] "YOU DO NOT MEAN TO KILL ME AS YOU KILLED THE EGYPTIAN YESTERDAY, DO YOU?" At this remark MOSES FLED, AND BECAME AN ALIEN IN THE LAND OF MIDIAN. . . . After forty years had passed, AN ANGEL APPEARED TO HIM IN THE WILDERNESS OF MOUNT SINAI, IN THE FLAME OF A BURNING THORN BUSH.

⁵¹EXODUS 3 & 4

3:6,10 Moses hid his face, for he was afraid to look at God. . . . [And God said,] "I will send you to Pharaoh, so that you may bring My people, the sons of Israel, out of Egypt." But Moses said to God, "Who am I, that I should go to Pharaoh?"

4:10-12 Then Moses said to the LORD, "Please, Lord, I have never been eloquent, . . . for I am slow of speech and slow of tongue."

⁵²ACTS 7

35-36 This Moses . . . is the one whom God sent to be both a ruler and a deliverer with the help of the angel who appeared to him in the thorn bush. This man led them out, performing wonders and signs in the land of Egypt and in the Red Sea and in the wilderness for forty years.

Moses was one with an unlikely background for his work. Born as a Hebrew slave in Egypt, he was destined for drowning by the king's edict. But God had other plans. Read Acts 7:21-24,26,28-30[50] and the verses from Exodus 3 and 4.[51] Circle "T" (true) or "F" (false) for each of the items below to indicate which circumstances (according to the Scripture passages) might have kept Moses from serving in his calling.

T	F	Born a Hebrew at a time when Hebrews were oppressed
T	F	Indoctrinated with idolatrous Egyptian ideas
T	F	Uneducated, ignorant
T	F	Poor
T	F	Viewed suspiciously by his own people
T	F	Physically weak
T	F	Spent years in exile
T	F	Looked down upon by the Egyptians
T	F	Not a good public speaker
T	F	Cowardly

Moses was more than a little handicapped from the beginning. He was of the wrong race and born at the wrong time. Those who saved his life infiltrated his mind with their idolatrous teachings and wicked ways. When he tried to defend one of his own, his own turned against him, making him a fugitive from justice. After forty years in the wilderness and nearing eighty years of age, Moses was fearful. He lacked confidence. But every phase of his life had been in preparation of his ultimate greatness before God.

Read Acts 7:35-36.[52] How does the New Testament writer sum up the life of Moses?

Moses was unique in his calling, but not unique in being called. We are each also gifted, and every Christian has an assignment in the kingdom of God. That calling isn't just for religious professionals. In fact, it is God's intention that most of us are to be in areas of ministry in secular locations. Our primary objective is to bring the light of His truth to a dark world.[T17]

How does the truth of your calling affect your sense of purpose? How does it bring new meaning into your work?

What we do and where we do it is extremely important to God. Achieving the work God has given us to do is what will give our work purpose and meaning.

Does your work satisfy you? Does it have purpose and meaning? If your work is unfulfilling, it may be because you are not operating in your calling. You may be doing the wrong type of work, you may be working for the wrong employer, or you may be focusing on the temporal rather than the eternal. Spend some time reflecting on your work in light of today's study.

BRINGING IT HOME

1. Where do you feel you are more nearly operating in your calling at your workplace: in the work of your mind and hands, or in fulfilling the Great Commission to win souls to the kingdom of God? How might you improve in your weaker area?

2. If you aren't operating as fully as you might in either your work or your workplace ministry, consider whether you might be suffering from fear of failure. If this seems to be a potential problem, ask God to help you determine the source of that fear. Think through issues such as rejection, inadequate training, timing, financial responsibilities, and so forth. Pray for God to empower you by His Spirit so that you might overcome any obstacles that are keeping you from following your calling.

POINT OF INTEREST:[T17]
A SECULAR JOB IS A MATTER OF MOTIVE—People in full-time Christian service can be just as vulnerable to wrong motives for working as can those in secular activities. Christian workers, for example, can be guilty of pursuing the visible over the invisible, and they can be on the same quest for power or success as anyone else. This happens in all kinds of ministries. People fall into the delusion that the empire they are building is for the glory of God when, in fact, it's to gain their own glory. First, their names become identified with the work. Then the growth of their empire is touted as evidence of God's blessing. At the same time, no little emphasis is being placed on the leader's charisma or leadership prowess. Ironically, in the height of their success such people are usually blind to what everyone else sees clearly.

All Christian vocations become secular the minute the focus of the Christian worker's heart is set on the temporal, that is, when his or her work is set apart *from* rather than *to* God. Likewise, secular work becomes spiritual when the worker is doing it as unto the Lord and not to please or impress people. The difference is not determined by the environment or the activity, but by the inward desire of the heart. God is far more concerned with the direction and focus of our hearts than with what we do with our hands; for if our heart is right, our hand will follow.

DAY 4

DOES MONEY MATTER?

[53]**NUMBERS 27**

15-17 [Moses said,] "May the LORD . . . appoint a man over the congregation, who will . . . lead them out and bring them in, that the congregation of the LORD will not be like sheep which have no shepherd."

[54]**JOHN 10**

11-13 "I am the good shepherd; the good shepherd lays down His life for the sheep. He who is a hired hand, and not a shepherd, who . . . sees the wolf coming, and leaves the sheep, . . . flees because he is a hired hand, and is not concerned about the sheep."

[55]**LUKE 16**

13-15 "No servant can serve two masters; for either he will hate the one and love the other, or else he will be devoted to one and despise the other. You cannot serve God and wealth." Now the Pharisees, who were lovers of money, . . . were scoffing at Him. And He said to them, "You are those who justify yourselves in the sight of men, but God knows your hearts; for that which is highly esteemed among men is detestable in the sight of God."

[56]**DEUTERONOMY 28**

8 The LORD will command the blessing upon you in your barns and in all that you put your hand to, and He will bless you in the land which the LORD your God gives you.

We learned in yesterday's study that everyone is born with certain gifts and talents that need to be fully developed and prayerfully utilized. Yet few people follow God's leading in their career choices. One reason is their fear that God may call them into a field that will not support the lifestyle they have in mind.

If money is our culture's exchange medium for even our basic provision, then salary is certainly not irrelevant. However, most of us are so conditioned to the ways of the world that even Christians find it difficult to know what part salary should play in a biblical career decision.

Suppose you were assigning a weight to individual career issues (job location, personal interest, family considerations, and so forth). On the chart below, check what percentage you would assign to salary or income potential.

__0%   __10%   __25%   __40%   __50%
__60%   __75%   __80%   __100%

Let's begin our examination of money issues by looking at a hypothetical job in the religious work arena. Suppose an interviewing pastor said to the steering committee, "Before I take this position, you need to know that I'll expect to earn a good salary here, with annual pay increases. I'll also be pursuing some well-paying speaking engagements on the side. If you'll do your part, then I'll remain your pastor—unless, of course, I get a significantly better offer." If you were part of that committee, would you vote to hire this person as your pastor? Why or why not?

Certainly a pastor and his family should be well cared for by the church he serves. But to demand a high standard of living at the spiritual expense of the church is not the mark of a true servant of God. Read Numbers 27:15-17[53] and John 10:11-13.[54] One appointed over the congregation is compared to what? Draw a symbol to represent that profession.

How is a shepherd different from a hireling?

The term "pastor" is tied metaphorically to a shepherd—one who tends and protects the sheep. Our hypothetical pastor is obviously more concerned about money than about the flock of God. Would he be considered a shepherd or a hireling?

Let's imagine another hypothetical interview. Suppose you are in a position to offer a job to a Christian business manager. He says to you, "I believe God would have me work for your company. But before I take this position, you need to know that I'll expect to earn a good salary here, with annual pay increases." Would that disqualify him for your position? Why or why not?

Rethink your interview of the Christian business manager in light of Luke 16:13-15.[55] What potential problem does this verse bring into question?[T18]

Both pastor and businessman in these scenarios are trying to operate with a dual allegiance, that is, both to God and to mammon (riches). According to these verses, however, such allegiance is impossible, for they are opposed to one another. What is the difference between people's view of riches and God's view of riches, according to Luke 16:13-15?

Read Deuteronomy 28:8[56] and Job 42:10,12.[57] What form does God's blessing take?

Under the Old Covenant (Testament), material prosperity was seen as an indicator of God's approval; it was Israel's reward for obedience and righteousness. But most of the Old Testament is best understood as a picture or "type"—that is, a physical expression that foreshadows what would become a spiritual reality in the Messiah (Christ). That which was foreshadowed in the Old Testament is realized in the New; namely, the reward for obedience and righteousness is the spiritual prosperity that

POINT OF INTEREST:[T18]
ALL CHRISTIANS ARE IN FULL-TIME MINISTRY—If you're a Christian, your work is an arena for, and an expression of, your ministry. This is not an option. Those in a secular place of ministry focus their workday on the objectives of their employers. But they advance the kingdom by example and by making the most of opportunities to share the good news. They are sent out as salt and light to a people in darkness. Those in religious ministries focus on seeing to the physical, emotional, and spiritual care of the body of Christ (the church). Their job is to equip those who minister in the secular workplace and community.

Christians who minister in religious workplaces have the same struggles and conflicts that face Christians who minister in secular workplaces. Both struggle with rightly dividing up their time among various responsibilities, tending to their vision for ministry, and fulfilling their roles and responsibilities toward their families. Both have to determine where and how to set boundaries and limits so that their efforts result in the maximum effectiveness for kingdom purposes. Both will feel the pressures of the limits of time and energy and will face the temptation to cut short the time needed to nurture their relationship with God.

If you are a Christian who ministers in the secular workplace, you must not have the attitude that advancing the kingdom is the work of the clergy. You are a soldier and a servant in God's kingdom. The only question is how and where you'll serve.

[57]**JOB 42**

10,12 The LORD restored the fortunes of Job when he prayed for his friends, and the LORD increased all that Job had twofold. . . . The LORD blessed the latter days of Job more than his beginning.

[58]**1 TIMOTHY 6**

10 For the love of money is a root of all sorts of evil, and some by longing for it have wandered away from the faith and pierced themselves with many griefs.

[59]**HEBREWS 13**

5 Make sure that your character is free from the love of money, being content with what you have; for He Himself has said, "I WILL NEVER DESERT YOU, NOR WILL I EVER FORSAKE YOU."

[60]**JEREMIAH 22**

13 Woe to him . . . who uses his neighbor's services without pay and does not give him his wages.

[61]**MALACHI 3**

5 "I will draw near to you for judgment; and I will be a swift witness . . . against those who swear falsely, and against those who oppress the wage earner in his wages, . . ." says the LORD of hosts.

[62]**1 TIMOTHY 5**

17-18 The elders who rule well are to be considered worthy of double honor, especially those who work hard at preaching and teaching. For the Scripture says, "YOU SHALL NOT MUZZLE THE OX WHILE HE IS THRESHING," and "The laborer is worthy of his wages."

[63]**GENESIS 31**

4-7 (see page 141)

is ours in Christ. John writes, for example, "Beloved, I pray that in all respects you may prosper and be in good health, just as your soul prospers" (3 John 1:2).

According to our Lord's words in Luke 16:15, the things that people esteem highly God finds detestable. "Detestable" (*bdelugma* in the Greek) comes from the root word *bdeo,* meaning "to stink."

Read 1 Timothy 6:10[58] and Hebrews 13:5.[59] About what are we warned in these passages?

Money itself is neutral. Loving money is not. Having wealth is neutral. Pursuing wealth is not. Wealth becomes detestable to our Lord when we esteem it more highly than we esteem Him, or when we pursue it at the expense of relationships—with God and others.

In light of what we've seen so far, it may appear that salary should be of no concern to us at all. Read Jeremiah 22:13,[60] Malachi 3:5,[61] and 1 Timothy 5:17-18.[62] How do these verses bring balance to the issue of compensation?

Whether the work is in a religious or secular environment, God sternly condemns taking financial advantage of the worker. Any business *or* ministry that survives only by taking advantage of its employees should not survive at all. Somewhere there is serious error. This is especially so if the business owner(s) or those in charge of ministries are living well, even extravagantly, at the expense of everybody else.

Now suppose you feel called to a certain workplace in spite of obvious wage injustices and abuses of power there. Do you think you should obey or reject the call? Why?

__ Obey because:

__ Reject because:

What insight do you gain from Genesis 31:4-7?[63]

God could very well be sending you into an oppressive place of employment to be salt and light. Light exposes truth, which may be what is needed in the face of corruption. And, like Jacob, you may be ill treated or even persecuted. Nevertheless, the Lord will protect you from harm and will provide for you in other ways until He lifts you out of that situation. You need not fear. God protects those who are His. Ultimately, God will not allow you to be hurt.[T19]

BRINGING IT HOME

1. Is the pursuit of wealth a stumbling block for you in your Christian walk? How is this manifested in your life? How does it affect your giving? Do you help support those who work directly in Christian ministries?

2. Are you seriously underpaid in your work? If so, consider the reason for your circumstance. Were you called to work in this business or ministry? How is God meeting your needs apart from your employer? If you've not been called to this work arena, what are you going to do to begin finding the place where God wants you to serve? Put a date on your calendar to begin your first step.

POINT OF INTEREST:[T19]

GOD'S SAFEKEEPING—One of the greatest fears people face is the loss of income or material possessions. But such fear loses its power when the Christian takes into account the faithfulness of God. That the Lord will never leave or forsake us is the most comforting knowledge we can have. People may reject or mistreat us, positions may come and go, money may be fleeting, but the lovingkindness of the Lord, expressed in relationship with Christ, is certain.

He who extends to you forgiveness, acceptance, and love is like the parent who has the child's hand in a tight grip before they cross the street. The Lord knows how to hang on to us! If we truly belong to Him, He won't let us stray far before He puts pain in that route. God's severe mercies will get our attention. A raw pagan will have more enjoyment out of life than a child of God who is straying from his or her walk with Him. No one is more miserable than a true believer who is out of step with the Father.

SCRIPTURE MEDITATION

"Observe how the lilies of the field grow; they do not toil nor do they spin, yet I say to you that even Solomon in all his glory clothed himself like one of these. But if God so clothes the grass of the field, which is alive today and tomorrow is thrown into the furnace, will He not much more clothe you?" (Matthew 6:28-30)

DAY 5

WHAT IS OUR SPIRITUAL CALLING?

Sooner or later, even non-Christians come to realize that the work of their hands (or of their minds) is, and has always been, futile. Realizing that one's life pursuit has been meaningless is painful, and it can lead to bitterness or despair. Yet God does not intend for us to expend our mental and physical energies on futile efforts. Instead, He calls us to elevate our work by performing it with an eye toward His agenda.

Read John 5:19-20.[64] What kind of works did Jesus (our role model) do?

God has been working to redeem a lost world. Jesus—God the Son—came into the world to do what He saw God the Father doing, namely, reconciling people to God. What was the heart relationship between the Father and the Son, according to this passage in John?

Jesus placed value on His own work according to the degree that His work contributed to the Father's goal and to the extent that His work was accomplished in loving relationship to the Father. Our own work will attain purpose and value only when it is performed in vital relationship to Christ, with our eyes fixed on His goals as our work objective.

Read Philippians 2:5-8[65] and Hebrews 5:8.[66] What did Jesus give up, and what did He take on?

What did Jesus learn, and how did He learn it? To what point was He obedient?

It seems strange to read of Jesus needing to learn anything at all, but especially that He needed to learn obedience. Yet Scripture tells us that Jesus emptied Himself of His own divine prerogatives and willingly became bound by flesh and bone. In so doing, He became subject to learning through human suffering.

---

[64] **JOHN 5**
19-20 Jesus [said] . . . , "The Son can do nothing of Himself, unless it is something He sees the Father doing; for whatever the Father does, these things the Son also does in like manner. For the Father loves the Son, and shows Him all things that He Himself is doing; and the Father will show Him greater works than these."

[65] **PHILIPPIANS 2**
5-8 Have this attitude in yourselves which was also in Christ Jesus, who, although He existed in the form of God, did not regard equality with God a thing to be grasped, but emptied Himself, taking the form of a bond-servant. . . . Being found in appearance as a man, He humbled Himself by becoming obedient to the point of death, even death on a cross.

[66] **HEBREWS 5**
8 Although He [Jesus] was a Son, He learned obedience from the things which He suffered.

[67] **HEBREWS 2**
17-18 [Jesus] had to be made like His brethren in all things, so that He might become a merciful and faithful high priest in things pertaining to God, to make propitiation for the sins of the people. For since He Himself was tempted in that which He has suffered, He is able to come to the aid of those who are tempted.

[68] **1 PETER 4**
1 Since Christ has suffered in the flesh, arm yourselves also with the same purpose, because he who has suffered in the flesh has ceased from sin.

Read Hebrews 5:8[66] again and then Hebrews 2:17-18.[67] Why did Jesus have to walk out the human experience, including suffering and dying on a cross?

Though fully God and perfect in wisdom and knowledge, Jesus willingly accepted the "job" of the Savior of men, carrying out His duties even to the point of becoming God's own sacrificial Lamb.

Philippians 2:5-7 tells us to have the same attitude that Jesus had. Review the primary job title of all believers from page 38, then read instructions from 1 Peter 4:1[68] and 1 Peter 2:19,21.[69] Relate your spiritual calling to that of Christ by checking everything that applies to both Christ and the believer.

____ Priestly service   ____ Has always been God

____ Willing to suffer   ____ Faithful example

____ A bond servant   ____ Overcomes temptation

____ Obedient to the   ____ Faithful
     point of death

____ Made substitutionary payment for our sin debt

Because only Jesus is (and has always been) God, He alone could make substitutionary payment (propitiation) for the sins of all humankind. But under the High Priesthood of Jesus, we also serve as God's priests to a lost world.[T20]

With Christ as our example, what works should we do as priests unto God? Read Luke 4:43,[70] 1 John 3:8,[71] 1 Timothy 1:15,[72] and John 17:4.[73] List the specific work God gave Jesus to do (that is, His purpose):

If we follow the example of Jesus in doing the works of the Father, we must share the gospel, do battle with the devil, win sinners to Christ, and glorify God by completing the work He has given us to do. We must also share our Lord's attitude toward suffering, handling temptation,

HISTORY & CULTURE:[T20]

ISRAEL'S PRIESTHOOD—When God met with Moses on Mount Sinai, He established not only the Law but also a religious system by which lawbreakers could be made right with God. The system encompassed specific instructions for worship, and it included detailed directions for building and furnishing a portable tabernacle, carrying out an array of acceptable sacrifices for sin, and establishing Israel's priesthood.

Of the twelve tribes of Israel, God singled out the tribe of Levi to carry out priestly duties for the people. The priests acted as mediators, representing the people to God and being God's representatives to the people. The priests also served as teachers, interpreting the Law and ruling on matters of worship, giving, purity, and morality.

However, the nation of Israel was also to serve as a "priest" to the Gentile nations. Consider Exodus 19:3,5-6: "Moses went up to God, and the LORD called to him from the mountain, saying, 'Thus you shall say to the house of Jacob and tell the sons of Israel: . . . If you will indeed obey My voice and keep My covenant, then you shall be My own possession among all the peoples, for all the earth is Mine; and you shall be to Me a kingdom of priests and a holy nation.' These are the words that you shall speak to the sons of Israel."

The priesthood of the believer, then, is a concept that began not with Christianity, but with the beginning of God's separation of a people to Himself, that the whole world might be redeemed unto God.

For further study:
Exodus 20, 28, and 40

[69] **1 PETER 2**

19,21 This finds favor, if for the sake of conscience toward God a person bears up under sorrows when suffering unjustly. . . . For you have been called for this purpose, since Christ also suffered for you, leaving you an example for you to follow in His steps.

[70] **LUKE 4**

43 [Jesus said], "I must preach the kingdom of God to the other cities also, for I was sent for this purpose."

[71] **1 JOHN 3**

8 The Son of God appeared for this purpose, to destroy the works of the devil.

[72] **1 TIMOTHY 1**

15 It is a trustworthy statement, . . . that Christ Jesus came into the world to save sinners.

[73] **JOHN 17**

4 "I [Jesus] glorified You on the earth, having accomplished the work which you have given Me to do."

[74] **MATTHEW 6**

31-33 "Do not worry . . . , saying, 'What will we eat?' or 'What will we drink?' or 'What will we wear for clothing?' For . . . your heavenly Father knows that you need all these things. But seek first His kingdom and His righteousness; and all these things will be added to you."

showing mercy, being a faithful example—even being obedient unto death.

How does this spiritual calling of believers play out in the workplace?[T21] Read Matthew 6:31-33.[74] What is the purpose of work, according to the world's value system?

Unless we shift our focus to an eternal perspective, work has no purpose beyond basic provision—food, clothing, shelter—and accumulating material wealth. God does not negate the fact that we need these things, but He does redefine how we are to obtain them. Write God's plan below:

To find purpose and meaning in our work, we must always be about the duties of our primary job; namely, being a priest unto God who follows the example of Jesus, our High Priest. If we focus on the kingdom of God and His righteousness, our first desire will be to serve the King. Then our work will be as a fragrant offering lifted up to Him.

There's another benefit to working in relationship to the Father and working toward His goals and objectives. According to Romans 8:28-30,

> We know that God causes all things to work together for good to those who love God, to those who are called according to His purpose. For whom He foreknew, He also predestined to become conformed to the image of His Son, that He might be the first-born among many brethren; and whom He predestined, these He also called; and whom He called, these He also justified; and whom He justified, these He also glorified.

The ultimate equalizer in life is not based on time, talent, or treasure. The rewards in the kingdom of God are based on faithfulness to opportunities. When we grasp this truth, we will turn our gaze away from the work of our hands and will focus our hearts on the work of God's heart. We will be about the business of building up the kingdom of God and allowing God to meet our human needs.

BRINGING IT HOME

1. During our life on earth, God is preparing us for citizenship in heaven. Work is one of the tools He uses to conform us to His character, that is, to teach us love, joy, peace, patience, kindness, gentleness, and self-control. In turn, He uses people of godly character to manifest His image in the workplace.

   Think of the wide range of experiences that are common to the workplace. List some that come to mind and note how God might be using them as training for your own spiritual maturity.

Experience	Christlike Character

   Which character trait of Christ (from the above list) do you feel is most lacking in your life? Ask God to help you grow in that area and to refocus your heart on kingdom purposes.

POINT OF INTEREST:[T21]

HOW SIGNIFICANT ARE OUR CAREER CHOICES? —Often we don't spend enough time contemplating God's plan for our lives or thinking through our career decisions. Our career choices affect where and how we will live. We may choose a career for personal satisfaction, knowing that the salaries are relatively low. Or we may select a career on the basis of its financial rewards and find ourselves materially prosperous and vocationally miserable.

Even if we like our jobs and are well paid, there will be a nagging sense of unfulfillment if it isn't in line with God's plan for our lives. Rarely are we short on ideas of what we'd like to do or how we'd like to live, and God often gives us the opportunity to bring those ideas to fruition. But what will be missing from our lives will be the deep satisfaction that comes only from obedience and the joy of being used by God.

SCRIPTURE MEDITATION

By grace you have been saved through faith; and that not of yourselves, it is the gift of God; not as a result of works, so that no one may boast. For we are His workmanship, created in Christ Jesus for good works, which God prepared beforehand, so that we would walk in them. (Ephesians 2:8-10)

To the leader: You will need sheets of paper and pens or markers for activity 5.

1. As with so many other things, there's a proper balance to be achieved in the matter of our work. On the one hand, there are many good reasons to work; on the other hand, those same good motivations can be detrimental to our family life or spirituality.

   • Take a look at the following reasons for working and think about whether you, personally, have any additional reasons for working. Finally, rank all the reasons in the order of their motivating you to work.
   __Society expects people to work.
   __If I want food and shelter I *have* to work.
   __I have a drive to succeed.

   • Which is the bigger temptation for you: laziness or workaholism? Why? What are you doing about it?

   • Have you ever known a case where success in the business world led to pride or self-sufficiency in the heart of the "successful" person? If so, tell the story.

2. Some people have never heard of the idea that a person's work can be a "calling" from God. Others have heard about it but think that it pertains only to people in full-time religious work. In fact, any job can be a calling if that's the context where God wants you to serve Him.

   • How has your outlook on "calling" changed since completing this unit?

   • Read the following story about racing champion Jeff Gordon, and examine it for the ways it shows that racing is Gordon's calling. (Hint: Look for *natural gifts, shaping circumstances,* and *opportunities to exercise skill.*)

Jeff Gordon has many fans and some detractors, and all for the same reason—because he's so successful. His detractors claim to dislike him because his success has come too easily for him. But has it? It's true that he was born with that rare combination of quick reactions and quick thinking. But he has also been practicing since childhood, first in midget car racing, then sprint car racing, and finally by entering NASCAR events as early as he was allowed. Since becoming a Christian, Gordon has been a faithful and effective witness for the Lord in the prominent position where the Lord has placed him.

3. Something is not "sacred" just because it's overtly religious; nor is something "secular" just because it is not. For the Christian, everything is sacred if we are lifting up the Lord through it.

   • In what sense is a Christian a priest?

   • A saint of the past once said, "Share Christ at all times. If necessary, use words." How does this relate to our acting as priests in the workplace?

   • Are you satisfied in your work, feeling that it helps to give your life meaning? What does that say about whether you are working in the job to which God has called you?

4. Another area where we need balance is the area of money. Appropriate payment for work done is good; a constant lust for more is not.

   • If a Christian who is a manager were to take seriously her role as "shepherd" of her employees, how might that affect her ways of doing business?

   • What are some signs that a person's appreciation for money has crossed the line and become an ungodly pursuit?

   • If you were not being compensated fairly, what (if anything) would you do about it?

5. Though work can sometimes seem pointless, God wants to elevate our work by allowing us to serve His greater purposes in the midst of it.

   • Read Jesus' words in John 15:1-11. How can abiding in Him make us fruitful in the context of our work? Give specific examples.

   • On a sheet of paper, create a map that shows paths you have taken toward obeying God. Label key turning points, draw road signs, or design your map however else works for you. Use your map to share with others the insights you've gained about learning obedience.

   • "Heavenly rewards are based on faithfulness, not achievement." Do you agree or disagree with that statement? Explain why.

Close your group time with prayer. Thank God for leading members of your group into jobs where they can serve Him as He designed them to. If any group members are working in jobs that they think are not their calling, pray for each one, asking God to show them how to make the transition into the right kind of work.

INTRODUCTION TO UNIT 3
WORK AND IDENTITY

Destination: To become identified with our work instead of by our work.

My friend Frances isn't afraid to whack me when I (Gail) need it. Once she noted, "Every time you tell someone you're a writer, you push your hair behind your ear. Why do you do that?"

"Because," I answered, "that's what I do when I feel like I'm not quite telling the truth."

"You mean you *don't* write for a living?" she asked sarcastically. (Frances was getting her hammer ready.)

"Writing might be how I make my living," I said, "but a real writer has a degree in journalism or is published under her own byline or is at least acknowledged as a writer by another writer. I just don't have the right credentials to be a *real* writer, but when people ask me what I do for a living, I don't know what else to say."

I didn't really need Frances to point out the fallacy of my warped thinking. However, embracing truth didn't necessarily follow the knowledge of it. I kept stumbling over the fact that no human authority would have sanctioned me as a "real" writer based on a God-given ability. Apparently I, too, valued the approval of people over the gifting of God, and in so doing, I created a mental disconnect between what I did and who I was. The incongruity was miserable. Can you relate?

Of all the creatures on this planet, only we humans question our identity. In many significant ways, our work does help to define our identity, for work is an external manifestation of who we are. Our work should be the outworking of whatever mental abilities and creativity have been endowed to us by our Creator. In fact, when we're not operating in our giftedness, we often experience a nagging sense that something is not quite coming together for us.

While it is important for us to "do" what we "are," it is also important to recognize that work is but one dimension of our identity; it is not the whole or even the overriding expression of who we are. As Christians, our identity in Christ far transcends our identity in our work. We are children of the living God, fearfully and wonderfully made and deeply loved by the Father.

Being made in the image of God is the basis for all human worth and dignity; therefore, those who have based their identity on their job, job performance, or overall success have placed their security on a fragile foundation. Life is full of uncontrollable factors that can and will affect our careers. Some of those effects will be negative. Moreover, our work will eventually slip through our aging fingers. What then? If our value and worth have been measured by what we've done in the workplace, then we'll have no identity or value outside the work arena. It is this misplaced emphasis, in fact, that causes so many to experience an identity crisis at retirement.

As we study unit 3, we will look into issues on the relationship of work and identity, value and worth. Our goal is to learn to be identified *with* our good works without being identified *by* them.

[75]ISAIAH 64

8 O Lord, You are our Father, we are the clay, and You our potter; and all of us are the work of Your hand.

[76]ISAIAH 29

16 Shall the potter be considered as equal with the clay?

[77]ROMANS 9

14,21 There is no injustice with God, is there? May it never be! . . . Does not the potter have a right over the clay, to make from the same lump one vessel for honorable use and another for common use?

[78]GENESIS 12

1-3 The Lord said to Abram, "Go . . . to the land which I will show you; and I will make you a great nation, . . . and make your name great. . . . And in you all the families of the earth shall be blessed."

[79]EXODUS 36

1 Bezalel . . . and every skillful person in whom the Lord has put skill and understanding to know how to perform all the work in the construction of the sanctuary, shall perform in accordance with all that the Lord has commanded.

[80]JOSHUA 3

7 The Lord said to Joshua, "This day I will begin to exalt you in the sight of all Israel, that they may know that just as I have been with Moses, I will be with you."

DAY 1

SEEKING SIGNIFICANCE IN GIFTEDNESS

On day 2 of unit 2, we learned that our careers are not so much a matter of choice but a matter of calling. We are born with a predisposition toward those skills that will enable us to perform whatever work God has given us to do. This means, of course that, if we're operating in our field (or fields) of giftedness, we'll be more effective than we would be in fields where we have no natural aptitude.

Everyone is gifted, but not everyone is gifted equally—even in the same field. Does this seem unfair? Read Isaiah 64:8,[75] Isaiah 29:16,[76] and Romans 9:14,21.[77] What gives God the right to choose our level of giftedness?[T22]

One may be more skilled than another, but better skills are not always recognized or rewarded. Some, of course, may rise above their peers because their product or output is exceptional. But others will rise to prominence simply because they've had more opportunity to develop their talent, because they've received training from a prestigious institution, or because their social or political networks have provided them (or their work) with unusual exposure.

Read Genesis 12:1-3,[78] Exodus 36:1,[79] and Joshua 3:7.[80] Why were Abraham, Bezalel, and Joshua recognized? That is, why were they exalted in their calling?

Read Luke 12:42,48.[81] What responsibility is inherent in God's gifting and exaltation? Choose one of the following:

a. The responsibility to recognize and be proud of our gifting
b. The responsibility to achieve more than non-Christians
c. The responsibility to do the best with whatever we have been given

God will gift us in direct proportion to the degree of responsibility for which we will be held accountable. Therefore, we should not envy the skill or recognition of others in our field of expertise, nor envy those with skills we desire to have. Should God exalt us or bring recognition to our work, it will be for His kingdom purposes, just as it was with Abraham, Bezalel, and Joshua.

FAILURE TO USE ONE'S GIFTS

In the introduction to this unit, I (Gail) shared my struggles of not believing I was a "real" writer because I lacked the stamp of approval from a human institution. As I look back at my life, God's gifting for writing was actually evident in grammar school. By the time I began college, my writing was publishable (at least according to my English professors). Nevertheless, ten years went by before I pursued work in the writing field, and twenty years went by before I attempted to write anything for publication. Was this disregard for my gifting a sin in my life? Read Galatians 1:10.[82] What do you think, and why?

What may look on the surface like godly humility is often pride in an unusual costume. I didn't lack confidence in my skills so much as I feared criticism. Review Isaiah 64:8,[75] Isaiah 29:16,[76] and Romans 9:14,21.[77] In essence, what was I really doing in not using my gifts?

If the God of the universe fashions us in our mother's womb (Psalm 139) and consecrates us and appoints us to service before birth (Jeremiah 1), then we as clay vessels must not say to the Potter, "What do You think You're doing?" Who was I to disregard the gifts God had given me? After all, couldn't He open whatever doors I needed to serve Him through my talents and skills?

God finally exposed the unbelief and rebellion that hid behind my fear of criticism. One of the ways was through a letter by the late author Flannery O'Connor, printed in *Voices from the Heart*. She wrote to a friend:

> No matter how just the criticism, any criticism at all which depresses you to the extent that you feel you cannot ever write anything worth anything is from the devil, and to subject yourself to it is for you an occasion of sin. In you the talent is there and you are expected to use it. . . . You do not write the best you can for the sake of art, but for the sake of returning your talent increased to the invisible God to use or not use as He sees fit.

POINT OF INTEREST:[T22]

THE SOURCE OF OUR SKILLS—Today, farmers know how and when to plant, how and when to harvest, and how to preserve and prepare the produce. But have you noticed that even the people in the earliest Bible times had ways of doing these same things? They learned from the knowledge and wisdom passed down from one generation to the next and from their own discoveries in the practice of their work. Initially, however, the knowledge had to have come from God Himself. Both our innate skills and our accrued knowledge base are gifts from God.

In addition to our vocational skills and talents, Christians are given gifts for service in God's kingdom. Our spiritual gifts, given by God through the Holy Spirit, enable us to serve effectively in our ministry's calling. Some examples of gifts for practical service to the church (or the body of Christ) include giving, mercy, serving, teaching, encouragement, administration, and others. Scripture also mentions supernatural gifts, such as gifts of prophecy, healing, and discerning of spirits, to name a few.

We should be even more diligent to develop our spiritual gifts than we are our vocational gifts and talent. "As each one has received a special gift," Peter tells us, "employ it in serving one another, as good stewards of the manifold grace of God" (1 Peter 4:10).

Do you know what your spiritual gifts are? Are you using them in God's kingdom?

For further study:
Isaiah 28:23-29
1 Corinthians 12:1-31
1 Timothy 1:6

[81]**LUKE 12**

42,48 The Lord said, "Who then is the faithful and sensible steward? . . . From everyone who has been given much will much be required; and to whom they entrusted much, of him they will ask all the more."

[82]**GALATIANS 1**

10 Am I now seeking the favor of men, or of God? Or am I striving to please men? If I were still trying to please men, I would not be a bond-servant of Christ.

[83]**1 CORINTHIANS 4**

6-7 Learn not to exceed what is written, so that no one of you might become arrogant in behalf of one against the other. For who regards you as superior? What do you have that you did not receive? And if you did receive it, why do you boast as if you had not received it?

[84]**1 SAMUEL 2**

3 Boast no more so very proudly, do not let arrogance come out of your mouth; for the LORD is a God of knowledge, and with Him actions are weighed.

[85]**JEREMIAH 9**

23-24 Thus says the LORD, "Let not a wise man boast of his wisdom, and let not the mighty man boast of his might, let not a rich man boast of his riches; but let him who boasts boast of this, that he understands and knows Me, that I am the LORD who exercises lovingkindness, justice, and righteousness on earth; for I delight in these things," declares the LORD.

Resignation to the will of God does not mean that you stop resisting evil or obstacles, it means that you leave the outcome out of your personal considerations.

Take a moment to reflect on your life. Is there a skill that you've not developed because you've subjected yourself to criticism? Write it below:

Do you believe God is bigger than your fear? Check the response that most closely reflects your belief:

___ Absolutely   ___ For the most part
___ A little   ___ To be honest, no

God didn't gift us to put us on a shelf, but to use us to do good works. He is far bigger than our fears. Our responsibility, then, is to strive for excellence in the expression of our giftedness but to leave the outcome in God's hands.[T23]

BOASTING IN OUR ABILITIES

Being recognized for our abilities or being exalted because of our work can easily become a source of self-importance. Read 1 Corinthians 4:6-7[83] and 1 Samuel 2:3.[84] Why is self-exaltation foolish?

Self-exaltation is a real temptation for those who are exceptionally gifted or who have had unusual opportunities. But any temptation to pride can be mitigated by remembering that we've had no more to do with the degree of our aptitude or the strength of our skills than we've had with the size of our noses. We have simply received at God's hand the giftedness, the opportunities for honing our skills, and the place of employment where our gifts and training can be expressed—and that's no basis for boasting!

There's only one reason to boast. What is it, according to Jeremiah 9:23-24?[85]

The most important thing we can do is to understand and know the Lord. We must remember that, no matter how exceptional our giftedness, it will be insufficient as the source of our significance. Everything has been given to us by our Creator. As the work of His hands, we have no basis for self-promotion or for self-castigation—only for praise to

Almighty God, who has given great gifts to humankind. And in Him alone shall we boast.

BRINGING IT HOME

1. Some people know what their calling is from an early age. If you know you are in the right field and are following your calling, take a moment to thank the Lord for His direction and guidance.

2. If you've worked many years in what you feel has been the wrong career and believe you need a change, you may find the following exercise helpful.

    a. Divide a sheet of paper into three columns. Label the columns "Childhood Fun," "Adolescent Fun," and "Academic Fun." What things did you enjoy as a child? Were you good at building models, working puzzles, drawing or designing, dressing your dolls, inventing games, or perhaps even organizing your playmates? Write your answers in the "Childhood Fun" column.

    b. Make a similar list of your favorite fun things as an adolescent. Did you like sports, the drama club, home economics, dancing, helping your friends with problems, reading, or what? Write your answers under "Adolescent Fun."

    c. Under "Academic Fun," write your favorite subjects in high school or college. Note whether you use the skills gained from your favorite subjects in your job now.

    d. Call a close relative and a few close childhood or college friends. Ask them what they remember about your interests as a child or what they thought you were good at. List them under the appropriate column.

    e. Place your list before the Lord. Confess if you've been ignoring the Potter. Ask God to bring your gifts to the surface and show you what He wants you to do at this point. Trust His ability to guide you and to make His will known in your life.

POINT OF INTEREST:[T23]

THE PURPOSE OF OUR GIFTS—Our calling is not irrelevant; it has kingdom purposes. If we are attempting to work in our calling, therefore, we can expect the Enemy to discourage us with all kinds of evils and obstacles. He will suggest as the outcome our greatest fears, whether it's a fear of failure or a fear of the consequences of success. The way to move beyond fear is to refuse to dwell on the outcome. Stay in the present and see your work as a fragrant offering to God.

SCRIPTURE MEDITATION

What shall we say then? There is no injustice with God, is there? May it never be! For He says to Moses, "I WILL HAVE MERCY ON WHOM I HAVE MERCY, AND I WILL HAVE COMPASSION ON WHOM I HAVE COMPASSION." So then it does not depend on the man who wills or the man who runs, but on God who has mercy. (Romans 9:14-16)

DAY 2

SEEKING SIGNIFICANCE IN EDUCATION

Being skillful is highly esteemed in Scripture. Proverbs 22:29 asks, "Do you see a man skilled in his work? He will stand before kings; he will not stand before obscure men." While the biblical proverbs are not promises of God, they do represent (as we might say today) statistically significant probabilities. How might this proverb be applied or interpreted in our culture?

We learned in yesterday's study that each of us is born with certain natural aptitudes (or gifts). God gives us not only potential and interest in a given field but also the opportunities to hone our gifts through training and practice. Our part is to take full advantage of our opportunities and to strive for excellence in the process of learning and doing. Proverbs 22:29 is simply saying that people who highly develop their potential are far more likely to be recognized by "significant" others than those who don't.

According to Proverbs 1:5[86] and 9:9,[87] what characteristics enhance a person's capacity to learn?

The most basic ingredient for learning is teachability. Wise are those who know that they *don't* know, for education can begin only where we recognize our own deficiencies. As we seek wise counsel and gain understanding, we increase our capacity to learn even more.

It isn't hard to see how "wisdom," "wise counselors," and "understanding" would be prerequisites for education, but "righteousness" may not seem to fit. After all, even the unrighteous can learn, right?

The answer to that question is "yes and no." Read 2 Timothy 3:6-7.[88] What were the women always doing, and what always evaded them?

It doesn't take a lot of analysis to see how human knowledge can be antithetical to truth. We need only look at the sciences. Far too much of what was taught as fact even ten years ago has since been disproved. (And far too

---

[86]**PROVERBS 1**
5 A wise man will hear and increase in learning, and a man of understanding will acquire wise counsel.

[87]**PROVERBS 9**
9 Give instruction to a wise man, and he will be still wiser, teach a righteous man, and he will increase his learning.

[88]**2 TIMOTHY 3**
6-7 [False teachers] enter into households and captivate weak women weighed down with sins, led on by various impulses, always learning and never able to come to the knowledge of the truth.

[89]**PROVERBS 9**
10 The fear of the LORD is the beginning of wisdom, and the knowledge of the Holy One is understanding.

[90]**ECCLESIASTES 4**
4 I have seen that every labor and every skill which is done is the result of rivalry between a man and his neighbor. This too is vanity and striving after wind.

[91]**ECCLESIASTES 12**
11-14 The words of wise men are like goads, and masters of these collections are like well-driven nails; they are given by one Shepherd. But beyond this, my son, be warned: the writing of many books is endless, and excessive devotion to books is wearying to the body. The conclusion, when all has been heard, is: fear God and keep His commandments, because this applies to every person. For God will bring every act to judgment, everything which is hidden, whether it is good or evil.

much theory is taught as fact, such as macroevolution.)

The unrighteous can certainly be collectors of human-generated facts, but only the righteous can discern truth from error. Read 1 Corinthians 1:18–2:16 from appendix A. What do Christians have that is unavailable to unbelievers?

Read Proverbs 9:10.[89] What are the forerunners of wisdom and knowledge, according to these verses?

The fear of the Lord and the knowledge of God come through faith in Christ—the faith by which we are made righteous (1 Corinthians 1:30)—and are given by the Holy Spirit and the mind of Christ. Students at the very best colleges, then, may certainly learn, but they'll never come to the knowledge of truth apart from God. That's why it's so important to seek God's guidance in pursuing our education and training.[T24]

CHOOSING A COLLEGE AND A CAREER MAJOR

Instead of following God's leading, we often base our college and career choices on factors in the job market. If given the opportunity, we would seek degrees from prestigious colleges. And indeed, Ivy League colleges can typically enable students to land better jobs and demand significantly higher starting salaries than their peers with similar degrees from lesser known institutions. Furthermore, as a group, Ivy League graduates are also more likely to someday "stand before kings" (or maybe presidents). But are salaries, recognition, and a competitive edge biblically appropriate goals for us or our children?

Read Ecclesiastes 4:4.[90] Wise King Solomon wrote that every skill he had observed was motivated by what?

Apart from rebirth in Christ, both working hard and increasing one's skills are most often motivated by rivalry. The drive for the competitive edge can become obsessive, and the real cost of our education cannot always be recovered by higher starting salaries.

Read Ecclesiastes 12:11-14.[91] What is the outcome of excessive devotion to studies?

POINT OF INTEREST:[T24]

EDUCATION EXCESS—I (Gail) have the potential to be an education addict. One of my favorite T-shirt slogans is "So many books, so little time." This may seem like a lofty problem, especially to those who have never really enjoyed school or loved to read as a hobby. But, in truth, any good habit taken to excess can become a bad habit. It's far too easy to retreat into one's own internal world and miss the blessings of relationships.

Not all people who pursue advanced degrees do so out of a love of learning. Some continue their education, believing that higher and higher levels of training will compensate for their lack of self-confidence. However, there will never be enough information to make them feel adequate for their tasks. They need, instead, the confidence that comes with the assurance of God's calling. When God Himself has prepared us for our life's work, we can place our efforts into the hands of the only One who has any control over the outcome.

[92]**PSALM 78**

5,7 He established a testimony in Jacob and appointed a law in Israel, which He commanded our fathers that they should teach them to their children, . . . that they should put their confidence in God and not forget the works of God, but keep his commandments.

[93]**GENESIS 18**

19 I have chosen him [Abraham], so that he may command his children and his household after him to keep the way of the LORD by doing righteousness and justice, so that the LORD may bring upon Abraham what He has spoken about him.

[94]**LUKE 10**

38-42 [Jesus] entered a village; and a woman named Martha welcomed Him into her home. She had a sister called Mary, who was seated at the Lord's feet. But Martha . . . said, "Lord, do You not care that my sister has left me to do all the serving alone? Then tell her to help me." But the Lord answered and said to her, "Martha, Martha, you are worried and bothered about so many things; but only one thing is necessary, for Mary has chosen the good part, which shall not be taken away from her."

According to this passage, when all the facts are in, what is the conclusion? To whom does the warning apply?

Also according to Ecclesiastes 12:11-14, what is our every act going to be subjected to? Does this include our education?

It's difficult to bring balance into our lives during our college years. Every year we spend immersed in books is a year we put the rest of our lives on hold—careers, marriage, children, and even the work God may have called us to do. It's vitally important, therefore, to be sure of God's calling in our type, place, and degree of education.

ATTITUDE INVENTORY

Parents and teachers often try to guide young people into specific fields for various reasons. Check the top three criteria most would use as a basis of career choice:

___ Job security	___ Benefit to society
___ Work environment	___ Work close to home
___ Enjoyment	___ Freedom
___ Salary potential	___ Travel opportunities
___ Natural skill	___ Career of the future
___ Prestige	___ Other: _____

Consider the following situations, making a mental note of your "gut reaction" as you read:

1. God has called your bright child to an obscure campus to pursue a career that is typically low-paying.
2. God has called your daughter to a large, liberal college with a reputedly immoral campus.
3. God has called your bright son to a vocational school instead of college.

Most likely, at least one of these scenarios made you shudder. Nevertheless, God's call must be honored. If we help our children make college and career choices based on worldly values, then we will be sending them the message that their significance is found in academic credentials. Instead, we should be steering them toward the only education that really matters.[T25]

Read Psalm 78:5,7,[92] Genesis 18:19,[93] and Luke 10:38-42.[94] What "good part" will never be taken away?

If we are called by God to pursue higher education for kingdom service (as Ken was), then our training time will be well spent and the Lord will sustain us. But if we're operating on the basis of rivalry, we will misspend our time and energy and miss out on kingdom opportunities. Significance can't be found in intellectual pursuits, even from the halls of our most respected universities. Significance is found in learning at the feet of the Master. We may never stand before any earthly "kings," but with that "good part," we can go boldly into the throne room of the King of kings.

BRINGING IT HOME

1. Wherever God calls our children, we must celebrate that calling and be excited about how God will use them. Spend some time in prayer today, asking God to enable you to yield your own career or the calling of your child to His service.

2. Are any of the following areas potential stumbling blocks for you? If so, lift them up to the Lord, asking God to enable you to receive His choice for your life.

   a. Going to the mission field
   b. Choosing a blue-collar profession
   c. Attending a liberal college
   d. Entering a low-paying career field
   e. Being a stay-at-home mom

3. Are your academic credentials your own source of significance? Thank God for the opportunities you've been given and ask Him to give you a proper perspective and to help you look to Him for your significance.

POINT OF INTEREST:[T25]

EDUCATED BUT UNWISE— Never in the history of our country have so many people been educated on a college level and even have earned advanced degrees. Yet now, in the early days of the twenty-first century, Americans have a profound identity crisis. They amass a tremendous information base, but they don't know who they are or what their purpose in this life is. From a semicomatose state of disorientation, people are looking for their value in things that have no eternal significance.

Shortly out of college, couples are buying houses and cars that their parents could afford only late in their careers, if at all. Folks in every age group have more expendable income, more toys, and more assets than any previous generation. We are materially rich and emotionally and spiritually impoverished. And that trend will continue until our culture realizes that our significance is not based on *what* we achieve but in *whom* we believe.

SCRIPTURE MEDITATION

So that your faith would not rest on the wisdom of men, but on the power of God. . . . But just as it is written, "THINGS WHICH EYE HAS NOT SEEN AND EAR HAS NOT HEARD, AND WHICH HAVE NOT ENTERED THE HEART OF MAN, ALL THAT GOD HAS PREPARED FOR THOSE WHO LOVE HIM." For to us God revealed them through the Spirit; for the Spirit searches all things, even the depths of God. (1 Corinthians 2:5,9-10)

DAY 3

SEEKING SIGNIFICANCE IN PROFESSION

[95]**JAMES 2**
1,9 My brethren, do not hold your faith in our glorious Lord Jesus Christ with an attitude of personal favoritism. . . . But if you show partiality, you are committing sin and are convicted by the law as transgressors.

[96]**ACTS 10**
34-35 Peter said: "I most certainly understand now that God is not one to show partiality, but in every nation the man who fears Him and does what is right is welcome to Him."

[97]**PROVERBS 22**
2 The rich and the poor have a common bond, the LORD is the maker of them all.

"We hold these truths to be self-evident: That all men are created equal . . ." When we hear these words from our Declaration of Independence, our hearts swell with national pride. Do you believe that all people are created equal? If so, in what sense are they equal?

Let's begin today's study with a social quiz. Quickly rank the following positions by their probable social standing, beginning with "15" for the most respected job title.

___ Truck driver	___ Accountant	___ Teacher
___ Garbage hauler	___ Executive	___ Farmer
___ Librarian	___ Janitor	___ Politician
___ Receptionist	___ Engineer	___ Mechanic
___ Homemaker	___ Actress	___ Plumber

If you used our culture as your evaluative standard, you probably gave higher scores to the executive or the engineer (or perhaps even the actress) and lower scores to the homemaker, farmer, or garbage hauler. If so, you've just identified the American caste system, that is, our culturally sanctioned social ranking based primarily on differences in profession or occupation.

How does the idea of a caste system fit with your concept of all people being created equal?

We're sometimes disturbed when we recognize the deeply entrenched caste system in America because it doesn't fit the image of human equality that we pretend to believe. Nevertheless, most of us are well aware not only of the social strata that exist but also of the general location of our own rung on the social ladder.

Review 1 Corinthians 4:6-7[83] and 1 Samuel 2:3[84] on page 54. Do you think elevating one person over another on the basis of profession is simply a cultural norm, or could it be a spiritual problem? Why?

Look back at the occupations list and circle the top five occupations that are most necessary for the survival and well-being of our culture. Write the name and social ranking of each of these five occupations:

1.
2.
3.
4.
5.

What relationship do you find between the occupations most needed and the level of respect (and pay) afforded to people in those fields?[T26]

Does this strike you as just or fair? Why or why not?

As a group, manual laborers work harder, have less-desirable working conditions, and receive the least amount of money. At the same time, their services are often more vital to our society's well-being—even its very survival—than are the services of those we hold in higher esteem. It is ironic that the services we need the most are often the ones we least appreciate and reward. How do you think we arrived at this inverse value system?

Intellect and education are often cited as justification for our profession-based caste system. However, many crafts or trades (blue-collar jobs) are difficult to master, and high proficiency requires as much time as is required for a college degree. A better explanation is that a higher value for mental labor is generated by institutions that profit from that ideology. A sense of superiority is further perpetuated by the mental laborers themselves, whose positions give them power over the distribution of wages.

Partiality to the mental laborer affects not only the distribution of wages but also the perceived value of the individual. Read James 2:1,9,[95] Acts 10:34-35,[96] and Proverbs 22:2.[97] What does Scripture tell us about showing partiality?

POINT OF INTEREST:[T26]

SEEKING SUCCESS—We think a bright future begins with the right career path. We want an education at an Ivy League school, employment with a prestigious company, and all the trappings of having arrived (home, car, wardrobe), for the right image is important to continued advancement. Also important is hanging out with the right people and playing the right politics.

But we cannot pursue success in this way and be pleasing to the Lord. First, some of the actions that will be required of us on this path will really not be ethical (legal, perhaps, but not ethical). We'll be forced somewhere along the way to step on a few toes. Eventually, we'll probably end up stabbing one or more fellow workers in the back to gain a competitive edge over them. It's a vicious game, one that Christians should not engage in.

The only thing we should seek to succeed in is pleasing God. And, if we succeed in this effort, everything else will fall into its right and proper place in our lives.

[98]**MARK 6**

2-3 [Jesus] began to teach in the synagogue; and the many listeners were astonished, saying, ". . . Is not this the carpenter, the son of Mary?"

[99]**ACTS 18**

3 Because he [Paul] was of the same trade, he stayed with them . . . ; for by trade they were tentmakers.

[100]**1 CHRONICLES 17**

7 Say to My servant David, "Thus says the LORD of hosts, 'I took you from the pasture, from following the sheep, to be leader over My people Israel.' "

[101]**COLOSSIANS 4**

14 Luke, the beloved physician, sends you his greetings.

[102]**MATTHEW 4**

18 Walking by the Sea of Galilee, He saw . . . Peter, and Andrew his brother, casting a net into the sea; for they were fishermen.

What is the common bond between the rich and poor and (by conclusion) between those who are called to work with their minds and those called to work with their hands?

It's amazing how much of the world's thinking we can embrace without ever considering its impact on our Christian walk. God has consecrated us from birth, and He has equipped us and ordained us to serve Him in our places of work. Because God is Himself impartial, nobody can claim any justifiable superiority on the basis of the type of work God has called them to do or on their place of service.

There is no devaluing of manual laborers in the Bible. In fact, all Jewish children (even of the wealthy) had to learn a trade by which they could support themselves. What kinds of work did Bible heroes do? Read Mark 6:2-3,[98] Acts 18:3,[99] 1 Chronicles 17:7,[100] Colossians 4:14,[101] and Matthew 4:18,[102] then fill out the following chart.

Bible Hero	Occupation

Though some professions were considered dishonorable in the Jewish culture (such as tax collecting and prostitution), all honorable professions were esteemed. The Old Testament tells us that, among the Bible heroes, Adam was a farmer, Abraham was a rancher, and Joseph was an administrator. Peter was more than a fisherman, for he owned a boat (a sign of relative wealth) and a thriving fishing business. Paul helped support his own missionary work by tentmaking. Even the Lord Jesus, though an itinerant preacher, was a carpenter.[T27]

God is not impressed with our titles, no matter how much the world esteems us. We will never find significance in our professions, our job titles, or even our products. But we will find significance as we do our own work heartily as a sacrifice to the Lord. We will also find it in celebration of the diversity of skills God has given (both mental and manual) so that the full range of our earthly needs can be abundantly met.

BRINGING IT HOME

1. Are you in a profession that the culture holds in high esteem? Does that profession give you a sense of personal value? Be honest. Do you see others who are in socially devalued professions as inferior to you? If so, confess that to God and ask Him to give you a heart of humility.

2. Have you hired anyone to do manual labor that you either couldn't do or didn't want to do yourself? How did you compensate him or her? Was there a fair ratio between what you make per hour and what you were willing to give the manual laborer per hour, or did you adopt society's system in devaluing that person's work? If you show partiality by elevating the worth of your work while devaluing the work of others, confess that as sin and ask God to give you a new perspective.

3. Are you aware of any specific areas in your work where you tend to respond with pride and arrogance? How about in your home? List these areas below, then pray for God to increase your awareness to the point of making you uncomfortable until that bondage is broken.

4. If you are a manual laborer, do you feel inferior to those who are mental laborers? Do you avoid people in the church who are mental laborers? If so, confess the sin and ask God to give you confidence in His calling. If you're not sure you are in His calling, ask Him to reveal His direction for your life.

HISTORY & CULTURE:[T27]

CRAFTS AND TRADES IN ANCIENT ISRAEL—There were a number of crafts and trades in Israel according to ancient writings. Rabbis mention nail makers, bakers, tailors, sandal makers, and master builders among the various skilled laborers. Trade guilds existed fairly early in Israel, even in Old Testament times.

In some cases, a trade violated a religious, moral, or ethical principle. Tanning, for example, was looked down upon because the process forced one to handle dead animals—an act that the Jewish law condemned as unclean. The position of tax collector was reputed to be held only by schemers and swindlers. In general, however, craft workers were held in high esteem among the Jews during Jesus' time.

The level of respect held by craftsmen and artisans was an Israeli custom during Jesus' time. All the citizens were expected to rise to their feet when a scholar approached. But craft workers were so highly regarded that they were exempt from this requirement.

SCRIPTURE MEDITATION

I again saw under the sun that the race is not to the swift and the battle is not to the warriors, and neither is bread to the wise nor wealth to the discerning nor favor to men of ability; for time and chance overtake them all. (Ecclesiastes 9:11)

DAY 4

SEEKING SIGNIFICANCE IN POWER

As giftedness and educational opportunities are catalysts for worldly success in our culture, so money and power are its ultimate rewards. We may still esteem the rural doctor and the starving artist, but each one's credibility will go up with increased income or with a position of power.

Money and power are inseparable. One has the ability to produce the other, and both are required for greatness in the eyes of the world. In today's study, we'll be focusing on issues related to power and greatness, leaving money issues to be covered in greater detail in unit 4.

Let's begin by defining power. Use the word POWER to develop an acrostic of descriptive words illustrating power, each starting with one of the letters in the word.

P

O

W

E

R

Power can be associated with position, pushiness, ownership, oppression, wealth, wrangling, elitism, education, riches, rudeness, and so forth. Essentially, however, power is the ability to effect, actuate, or restrict change. In the workplace, power is the degree of control that a position holder has over others—primarily over their livelihood.[T28]

What seem to be the sources of power, both in society and in the workplace?

Workplace power is officially vested in position, but it can also be held vicariously. That is, power may stem from political affiliation with in-groups or with another person in authority. Power may also stem from the knowledge of or participation in subversive, corrupt, or perverted activities that may be going on behind the scenes.

Read 1 Chronicles 29:11-12[103] as well as Psalms 68:35 and 75:7.[104] To whom does power belong, and what is the extent of that power?

---

[103]**1 CHRONICLES 29**
11-12 Yours, O LORD, is the greatness and the power . . . , indeed everything that is in the heavens and the earth; Yours is the dominion, O LORD, and You exalt Yourself as head over all. . . . You rule over all and in Your hand is power and might; and it lies in Your hand to make great.

[104]**PSALM 68 & 75**
68:35 The God of Israel Himself gives strength and power to the people.
75:7 God . . . puts down one, and exalts another.

[105]**MATTHEW 23**
1-3 Jesus spoke . . . , saying, "The scribes and the Pharisees have seated themselves in the chair of Moses; therefore all that they tell you, do . . . , but do not do according to their deeds."

[106]**ROMANS 13**
1,4 Every person is to be in subjection to the governing authorities. For there is no authority except from God, and those which exist are established by God. . . . It [government] is a minister of God to you for good. . . . An avenger who brings wrath on the one who practices evil.

[107]**2 CORINTHIANS 10**
17-18 HE WHO BOASTS, IS TO BOAST IN THE LORD. For it is not he who commends himself that is approved, but he whom the Lord commends.

If all power in heaven and earth belongs to God, how do human beings gain power and greatness?

Sometimes God elevates men and women to power positions by direct or divine decree. Other times, people pursue power and God permits them to attain it, at least for a time, for reasons known only to Him. Whether God's power is extended to men and women by decree or by permission, however, He is still in ultimate control.[T29]

POWER PROFESSIONS

In addition to individual power positions, power in our culture can rest in a host of agencies (political, military, organized labor, and so on). In Scripture, however, God decrees broad authority and power over the working class to only two agencies. Read Matthew 23:1-3[105] and Romans 13:1,4.[106] What are the two agencies?

Why do you think God elevated the religious and government leaders?

God empowered religious leaders with authority to ensure the keeping of His moral law. God also empowered government with the authority to ensure the keeping of civil laws, that is, to maintain order and to marshal armies for the nation's protection.

Kings and priests were to rule in parallel over God's people and to serve as vicegerents under a theocratic headship. Yet religious as well as civil authorities were often tripped up by pride, taking honors due to the *position* as marks of their own *personal* greatness.[T30]

A self-assumption of greatness doesn't make one truly great. Read 2 Corinthians 10:17-18.[107] Who is approved? Who isn't?

Just as God has the sole storehouse of power, so also He has the sole storehouse of greatness, and He alone determines who will be great among people.

POINT OF INTEREST:[T28]

CORRUPTED POWER—Jeremiah wrote, "An appalling and horrible thing has happened in the land: The prophets prophesy falsely, and the priests rule on their own authority; and My people love it so! But what will you do at the end of it?" (5:30-31).

How clearly we can see the truth of these verses in our own society! Politicians are living in ways that cry out for God's judgment, but economists tell the people that business is doing great, so who cares? Apparently not the masses.

America is treading on dangerous ground and, as in the days of Noah, we are willfully blind to the consequences of sin and rebellion. Let it not be so with the people of God's kingdom.

POINT OF INTEREST:[T29]

HONOR IN POSITION—All human authority rests in position and is always limited by relationship and time. For example, a judge has power over people's lives only within the limits of the law (position) and only in his courtroom (power) and only during his tenure on the bench (time). A supervisor controls the activities of her subordinates only as they relate to the job (position) and only to the extent of her authority (power) and only during work hours (time).

The extent of human power will always be limited. However, there is not, has never been, and will never be any omnipotent (all-powerful) human being. Omnipotence rests in God alone, whose authority is not limited by position, power, or time.

[108] **GENESIS 12**

1-2 The LORD said to Abram, "Go forth from your country . . . , to the land which I will show you; and I will make you a great nation, and I will bless you, and make your name great; and so you shall be a blessing."

[109] **2 CORINTHIANS 4**

5,7 We do not preach ourselves but Christ Jesus as Lord. . . . But we have this treasure in earthen vessels, so that the surpassing greatness of the power will be of God and not from ourselves.

[110] **2 CORINTHIANS 12**

9-10 He has said to me, "My grace is sufficient for you, for power is perfected in weakness." . . . Therefore I am well content with weaknesses, with insults, with distresses, with persecutions, with difficulties, for Christ's sake; for when I am weak, then I am strong.

[111] **PSALM 18**

35-36 You have also given me the shield of Your salvation, and Your right hand upholds me; and Your gentleness makes me great. You enlarge my steps under me, and my feet have not slipped.

GREATNESS FROM GOD

All human greatness emanates from God, but people often take the glory for themselves. Consider some of the heroes recorded in Scripture. Read of Abraham's greatness, for example, from Genesis 12:1-2.[108] For what purpose did God make Abraham great?

God raised up Abraham to be the father of the nation through whom the entire world would be blessed. Both the Law and Jesus Himself came through Abraham's "seed."

Compare and contrast the greatness of two kings from Scripture (three kings are noted, but compare only David and Nebuchadnezzar for the following exercise). Read 2 Samuel 7:8-29, Jeremiah 25:8-12, Daniel 4:28–5:6,13-31, and Habakkuk 1:2-7,11,13 from appendix A. How do these kings compare in the following categories?

• **Their Self-Concept**
David (2 Samuel 7:18):

Nebuchadnezzar (Daniel 4:30):

• **God's Purpose for Their Greatness**
David (2 Samuel 7:21,26):

Nebuchadnezzar (Jeremiah 25:8-12 and Habakkuk 1:2-13):

• **God's Response to Their Humility/Arrogance**
David (2 Samuel 7:27-29):

Nebuchadnezzar (Daniel 4:31-32):

It seems right that God should exalt a person with a servant's heart like David's. But it's difficult to understand God's extending greatness to a king of an idolatrous nation. Nevertheless, God raised up Nebuchadnezzar of Babylonia (capital of Assyria) as His personal servant and used him to punish Israel so that they might repent and return to their God. Even Nebuchadnezzar came to realize that the Most High was the source of all power and greatness.

Like most everything, greatness is countercultural in God's kingdom. Read 2 Corinthians 4:5,7[109] and 12:9-10.[110] Why must Christians preach Christ in a spirit of meekness?

How is God's power perfected (or completed)?

Read Psalm 18:35-36.[111] What will make us great?

Greatness begins by accepting God's plan of salvation. But we will neither look to Him for salvation nor draw on God's strength until we recognize our sinfulness and our extreme human weakness. A new life in Christ begins when we empty ourselves and are filled with God's Spirit. It is the love of the Lord that draws us to repentance (Romans 2:4). It is His gentleness that makes us great.

BRINGING IT HOME

1. If you are in a position of power, perhaps as a parent or a leader in the church, ask God to reveal if you have expanded your territory beyond His intended limits or if you've failed to assume all the responsibilities of your assignment. Talk with both peers and subordinates and see if you need to make adjustments in your leadership style. Ask God to give you a teachable heart and the courage to make any important changes.

2. Do you have a new life in Christ? If not, or if you're not sure, read and meditate on the material in appendix B.

POINT OF INTEREST:[T30]

POWER WORKING—Many people engage in "power working"; that is, they are working powerfully in their jobs and in their office politics to gain a greater power position because, in their minds, their jobs are their identity.

If we allow our jobs to define us, then most of us will be like cogs in a large machine. Do you remember seeing the old film *Modern Times* with Charlie Chaplin? Chaplin gets swallowed up by a machine and we see his body going around and around on the cogs. The image is a wonderful metaphor of what work can be like if it's based on the temporal rather than on the transcendent.

When work defines us, we end up doing things a certain way just because we always have. We stop choosing. Our life becomes "whatever" as we take on a practice of reacting but never proacting. The difference is profound.

When we place our identity in Christ, He defines us from the top down and enables us to use our God-given reasoning ability to make choices that enhance not only our own lives but also the work of His kingdom.

SCRIPTURE MEDITATION

Thus says the LORD, "Let not a wise man boast of his wisdom, and let not the mighty man boast of his might, let not a rich man boast of his riches; but let him who boasts boast of this, that he understands and knows Me, that I am the LORD who exercises lovingkindness, justice and righteousness on earth; for I delight in these things," declares the Lord. (Jeremiah 9:23-24)

DAY 5

FINDING SIGNIFICANCE IN SERVICE

In this unit we've seen that personal significance cannot be found in giftedness, education, profession, or power. Yet the desire for significance remains a fundamental yearning deep in the soul of every human being. It is put there by God to drive us to Himself so that He might give us significance from His store of all-encompassing power, authority, and greatness (see 1 Chronicles 29:11-12).

Read Matthew 28:18.[108] How much of His authority and greatness did God extend to Jesus?

Jesus had all authority and power at His command, yet He used that authority and power in surprising ways. Read the following passages and note the attribute or behavior Christ demonstrated:

Passage	Attribute/Behavior
1 Peter 2:19,21[113]	
1 Timothy 1:15-16[114]	
Philippians 2:5-8[115]	
Matthew 11:29[116]	
Mark 10:45[117]	

These are neither the attributes nor the ways of behavior that the world would expect from omnipotence. Nevertheless, Scripture's account of the life of Jesus reveals over and over again that His unsurpassed humility and selflessness are at the heart of His unsurpassed greatness among men and women. And this is true even among those who do not yet bow their knee to Him.

God's perspective is always counter to our fallen human nature. Jesus didn't use His infinite power to impress or dominate others. Instead, He applied His powers toward obedience to the Father so that He might minister to people in humility and gentleness.[T31]

---

[112] MATTHEW 28

18 Jesus . . . spoke to them, saying, "All authority has been given to Me in heaven and on earth."

[113] 1 PETER 2

19,21 This finds favor, if for the sake of conscience toward God a man bears up under sorrows when suffering unjustly. . . . For you have been called for this purpose, since Christ also suffered for you, leaving you an example for you to follow in His steps.

[114] 1 TIMOTHY 1

15-16 Christ Jesus came into the world to save sinners, among whom I [Paul] am foremost of all. Yet for this reason I found mercy, so that in me as the foremost, Jesus Christ might demonstrate His perfect patience as an example for those who would believe in Him for eternal life.

[115] PHILIPPIANS 2

5-8 Have this attitude in yourselves which was also in Christ Jesus, who, although He existed in the form of God, did not regard equality with God a thing to be grasped, but emptied Himself, taking the form of a bond-servant. . . . Being found in appearance as a man, He humbled Himself by becoming obedient to the point of death, even death on a cross.

[116] MATTHEW 11

29 [Jesus said,] "Take My yoke upon you and learn from Me, for I am gentle and humble in heart; and YOU WILL FIND REST FOR YOUR SOULS."

[117] MARK 10

45 "The Son of Man did not come to be served, but to serve, and to give His life a ransom for many."

Jesus used His authority to bring the gospel to all people and to proclaim it boldly in spite of threats by lesser authorities and powers of evil. He accomplished the work of God by yielding His life as a ransom for the souls of men. Even those who were trying to oppose Him were Christ's unwitting accomplices. Even the power of death was a tool in His hand.

Read 1 Peter 2:19,21[113] again. What role should Christ's suffering play in our lives?

If Christ is our role model, how many of His attributes and behaviors should we emulate?

We cannot forgive sins or make anyone right with God. But we can emulate many of the attributes of Jesus' character, including His humility and selflessness. If those two attributes revealed the greatness of Jesus, what might they do for us? Read Matthew 20:27,[118] Luke 22:26,[119] Matthew 5:19,[120] and Luke 1:15-17.[121] What makes men and women great in God's kingdom?

The desire for autonomy and power is part of our inclination to sin. If we are indignant at servanthood, therefore, that's a good sign we don't have an eternal perspective. Perhaps we don't even know God. For in His economy, greatness comes through (1) serving others, (2) keeping and teaching God's commandments, and (3) being actively involved in turning people back to God.

Look at 1 Peter 2:9.[122] What job is described by these three activities? Whose job is this?

As Christians, our primary job on earth is to fulfill the duties of the priesthood of believers. Because we are sons and daughters of the King of kings, our priestly office is also a royal office. That means that both the moral and civil authority of God is vested in each of us by the Holy Spirit. We are thereby called and equipped to exercise that authority in our corrupted world.

Does that call seem overwhelming? Do you feel too weak to fulfill your royal duties? Do you tremble at the thought of such heavy responsibility? God understands.

HISTORY & CULTURE:[T31]

SIGNIFICANCE FROM GOD'S SERVICE—Jim Elliott, a missionary martyr killed in 1955 by the Auca Indians in Equador, said, "Wherever you are, be all there. Live to the hilt in any situation you believe to be the will of God."

This truth has major implications, not only for finding our significance in Christ, but also for balancing work and relationships. If you are working, then concentrate on what you are doing and work heartily at it. On the other hand, if someone is pouring out his or her pain to you and you feel God is using you in that person's life at that time, then be all there for the person. Don't let your mind flit to the other things you need to be doing, not even to your work. Don't even think about what you should say. Listen and let God give you wise words of counsel or encouragement. To do otherwise is to live in the future at the sacrifice of a present opportunity. Invest each day wisely, with an eternal perspective, for it is precious and will never return.

118MATTHEW 20
27 "Whoever wishes to be first among you shall be your slave."

119LUKE 22
26 "The one who is the greatest among you most become like the youngest, and the leader like the servant."

120MATTHEW 5
19 "Whoever . . . keeps and teaches [my commands], he shall be called great in the kingdom of heaven."

121LUKE 1
15-17 He [John the Baptist] will be great in the sight of the Lord. . . . And he will turn many of the sons of Israel back to the Lord their God. It is he who will . . . TURN THE HEARTS OF THE FATHERS BACK TO THE CHILDREN, and the disobedient to [righteousness].

1221 PETER 2
9 You are A CHOSEN RACE, A royal PRIESTHOOD, A HOLY NATION, A PEOPLE FOR God's OWN POSSESSION, so that you may proclaim the excellencies of Him who has called you out of darkness into His marvelous light.

123PHILIPPIANS 2
12-13 My beloved, just as you have always obeyed, not as in my presence only, but now much more in my absence, work out your salvation with fear and trembling; for it is God who is at work in you, both to will and to work for His good pleasure.

1242 TIMOTHY 4
5-8 (see page 141)

Read Philippians 2:12-13.[123] Who will be doing the work in you? Why?

We need not fear or be overwhelmed. The Lord Himself is working in us. His right hand upholds us; our feet will not slip. We can joyfully accept our commission as did His disciples, whom He commanded, "Go therefore and make disciples of all the nations, baptizing them in the name of the Father and the Son and the Holy Spirit, teaching them to observe all that I commanded you; and lo, I am with you always, even to the end of the age" (Matthew 28:19-20).

We can experience God's greatness through serving others and giving our lives for the things that have eternal value. Our Lord will never leave us. So no matter where our position is on the social ladder (the street sweeper or the CEO), the believer (as a royal priest) can rely on God's power and authority in his or her role of servant leadership. In all of life, there is no position of greater significance than serving Christ by serving others.

GOD'S RETIREMENT PLAN

Christians in all professions regularly apply the culture's vocational retirement concept to their work for the Lord. It's amazing, in fact, how many people in the church become "unavailable" when they retire from their vocations. Reasons range from wanting to be free to travel to wanting to spend more time with grandchildren.

Read of Paul's work in God's kingdom in 2 Timothy 4:5-8.[124] At what point in life was he writing to Timothy?

What was waiting for Paul on the other side of this life that will also be waiting for all who love Christ's appearing?

Our particular service in the kingdom will probably change with age, and God may even call us to invest more time in our families. But there is no place in Scripture where God relieved any of His servants from duty this side of heaven. We must work where we are called, regardless of our own personal interests. And we must work until God calls us home.

The Lord's assignment may allow us the freedom to travel or visit family—but it may not. Retirees are just as accountable to the Lord for manning their duty stations until God releases them as are young people. Therefore, we must be wise to the snares of the enemy, even in our senior years.

BRINGING IT HOME

1. If you are in a power position, know that you have been placed there for servant leadership. Ask God to show you how to serve those who are under your leadership in a way that will turn people to Him. Be careful to live in such a way that you reflect the heart of God before those whom you serve in leadership.

2. List the places God has called you to serve at your local church and/or in your community. Commit to God to remain at your place of duty until He releases you or moves you to another ministry.[T32]

3. If you are retired and have left the work of God's kingdom, you may be out of the will of God. Ask God to direct you and to show you where He would have you plug back into service in your church or community. Be willing to let the Lord stretch you to serve in areas you never dreamed of.

POINT OF INTEREST:[T32]

GIVING GOD GLORY— Christians in difficult work situations are often unsure whether they are in a trial of their faith (to be endured) or whether God is nudging them to move forward. If you are in this situation, find one or two prayer partners and commit to praying together until God reveals His will in your situation. If you are to stay in the job, ask Him to give you insight on how you might come through the trial, bringing glory to Him.

SCRIPTURE MEDITATION

What does the LORD your God require from you, but to fear the LORD your God, to walk in all His ways and love Him, and to serve the LORD your God with all your heart and with all your soul, and to keep the LORD's commandments and His statutes. (Deuteronomy 10:12-13)

And if it is disagreeable in your sight to serve the LORD, choose for yourselves today whom you will serve: . . . but as for me and my house, we will serve the LORD. (Joshua 24:15)

To the leader: You'll need a lamp and sheets of paper for the silhouette activity.

1. God's gifts to us (skills, abilities) are good things, but they are not where we should seek our significance. We should not neglect our gifts, but neither should we take personal pride in them.

   • Have you ever envied someone else's gift? Tell about that. How does knowing that God distributes gifts for kingdom purposes help you when you're tempted to be envious?

   • Have you ever neglected one of your gifts out of fear or for some other cause? Share with the others about that experience.

   • On page 54 we read, "We've had no more to do with the degree of our aptitude or the strength of our skill than we've had with the size of our noses." Take turns drawing the silhouettes of each other's noses (you'll need a lamp and sheets of paper taped to the wall). Have fun comparing the shapes and sizes of your respective noses. Then, if taking credit for your gifts is a temptation for you, take your nose silhouette home with you as a reminder of how silly that tendency really is.

2. Education is no better as a source of significance than is giftedness. There are many ways to get an education, and all of them can be good, but Christians should see themselves first of all as students of Jesus.

   • Pretend that you are advising a high school senior who is wondering what kind of college to go to. Work with others in the group to produce a chart showing the pros and cons of different kinds of higher education. Then brainstorm some questions that the high school senior should ask herself (regarding spiritual maturity, career goals, and so on) to begin sensing where God might want her to go for college.

   • If you noticed that a Christian friend of yours was taking too much pride in his expensive, prestigious education, what would you say to him for the sake of his spiritual welfare?

3. Ultimately, our significance does not come from our profession (though many people seem to think otherwise). All honorable professions should be esteemed, and in any of them, God can be honored.

   • Take turns naming the kinds of jobs you have held in your lifetime. Which jobs are considered more prestigious, and which jobs are considered less prestigious? How can Christians battle prejudice in this area?

   • Have you ever known someone who had a sense of worthlessness after retiring? What does this say about investing our sense of significance in our work?

4. Many people think that acquiring power over other people is what makes them great. But we have only to look at the example of Jesus to see that power is not to be used selfishly.

   • Share your POWER acrostic (page 64) with the others in the group.

   • Give an example of someone who was power-hungry. What do you think made him or her this way? What did the pursuit of power do for this person in the end?

   • Describe how Jesus used His power.

5. Significance can be found neither in giftedness nor in education nor in profession nor in power. It *can*, however, be found in service to others in Jesus' name.

   • Flip through the Gospels and try to identify a variety of ways that Jesus served other people. Shout it out when you've found one.

   • What person (someone you have known personally) best exemplifies servanthood for you? Why?

   • What makes serving others so hard? How can Christians grow in servanthood?

End your time together with a prayer in which you ask for God's help to stop seeking significance in all the wrong places and start finding it in Christian service. Pray also about specific ways group members want to begin serving others in their work arenas.

Introduction to Unit 4
Work and Wealth

Destination: To understand the relationships between our work and our prosperity.

I (Ken) was a boy of five or six when one night, before going to bed, I asked God to grant one request, namely, to put one million dollars in my wardrobe. I had heard about faith and praying without doubting. When I went to sleep that night, I had no doubts at all that my prayer, offered in faith, would be granted. The following morning I got out of bed, slowly walked to my wardrobe, and excitedly opened the door. My crushing disappointment at seeing nothing but clothes and shoes killed my "prayer life" for years. Without God as my cosmic slot machine, I was forced to build my "wealth" like the rest of humankind—by diligent labor.

Cervantes said that diligence is the mother of good fortune. We might translate this saying as "the harder we work, the luckier we'll get." This is not necessarily so, of course, but it's how we think nonetheless. For some, work is a means of personal significance—an arena for success and power. For most of us, however, work is the vehicle that enables us to live (or to sustain the hope of living) the lifestyle we desire. Toward that end, we work long and hard, then longer and harder, until pretty soon the only lifestyle we're experiencing is a wearisome grind. We reach burnout long before we reach Utopia.

Why haven't we been able to meet our financial goals? Perhaps we have set those goals without consulting the Father's plans for us. Or perhaps along the way those goals have become idols in our lives and, in pursuit of them, we have allowed our work to shape us instead of us shaping our work. Perhaps we have gotten our priorities out of kilter or have lost sight of the precious things in life—like our walk with God or our relationships with our families. Our loving Father will keep us from sacrificing the eternal on the altar of the temporal.

This scenario of failure will not apply to all. You may be one who has met your financial goals but found them to be empty and hollow. At times you feel like you've got the world in your hands, and all you really want is someplace to lay it down. You're tired of it all, but your life is so entangled that you can't find a way to get free from it. God is teaching you something too. He's allowing you to accumulate but not enjoy the things for which you've worked so hard. He wants you to learn experientially that the aching void you've been trying to fill with this world's goods cannot be satisfied by anything but Himself.

For those of you somewhere in between, take heed. If you've made wealth your goal, you'll eventually experience one of these two options. In pursuit of success, your job will demand so much of your time and energy that you won't be able to cultivate the things that make life worth living. The goal of the study in unit 4 is to give you guidance from God's Word on setting work boundaries and reassessing the priorities of your life. May you experience the true riches found only in Christ.

DAY 1

WORK AND PROFIT

[125]**ISAIAH 48**

17 Thus says the LORD, your Redeemer, the Holy One of Israel; "I am the LORD your God, who teaches you to profit, who leads you in the way you should go."

[126]**PROVERBS 13**

11 Wealth obtained by fraud dwindles, but the one who gathers by labor increases it.

[127]**PROVERBS 14**

23 In all labor there is profit, but mere talk leads only to poverty.

[128]**PROVERBS 30**

8-9 Give me neither poverty nor riches; feed me with the food that is my portion, that I not be full and deny You and say, "Who is the LORD?" Or that I not be in want and steal, and profane the name of my God.

[129]**ECCLESIASTES 5**

13 There is a grievous evil which I have seen under the sun: riches being hoarded by their owner to his hurt.

[130]**PROVERBS 23**

4-5 Do not weary yourself to gain wealth, cease from your consideration of it. When you set your eyes on it, it is gone. For wealth certainly makes itself wings, like an eagle that flies toward the heavens.

[131]**PROVERBS 27**

24 Riches are not forever, nor does a crown endure.

Christians are often criticized for attempting to make a profit, as if profit and wealth were evil or sinful. What does Scripture teach about profit? Read Isaiah 48:17.[125] How does the Lord God describe His role in regard to profit in our lives?

God doesn't just approve of our profiting from our labors; He initiated the process. We learned from Isaiah 28:23-26[8] (page 18) that God Himself taught men and women how to apply their own gifts and talents in creative labors. He also provided an environment so rich in resources that people soon learned to produce more than they needed. The excess became valuable products that could be exchanged for the creative labors of others.

The Hebrew word for "profit" used in Isaiah 48:17 is *yaal,* which means "to confer or gain profit or benefit." The broad implications of this word encompass more than just material increase. In what other ways might we profit or benefit by interchanges in the marketplace?

Work is more than just an arena for increasing our financial holdings; it is one of God's mechanisms to bring us together in community. Within the context of product and labor exchanges, we can also (1) increase the quality of our relationships (with God and with others), (2) increase our collective potential for significant achievements, and (3) increase our opportunities for living out and sharing the gospel in a neutral and natural environment.

Read Proverbs 13:11[126] and 14:23.[127] By what means does God intend for us to profit financially?

Proverbs 14:23 uses a different Hebrew word for "profit" from labors. Here "profit" *(mothar)* means "abundance; preeminence." *Mothar* comes from the root word *yathar,* meaning "to remain over." This verse tells us our labors should produce an abundance, with some to spare.

THE DESIRE FOR PROFIT

Profit, as God intended it, certainly isn't sin. The human problem with profit, however, is that we're prone to seek profit for profit's sake. We make it an obsession—one that can take us down any number of paths toward sin. What fundamental sins or temptations do you see in Proverbs 30:8-9[128] and Ecclesiastes 5:13?[129]

Read Proverbs 23:4-5,[130] 27:24,[131] and 11:28.[132] Why is the quest for wealth a bad financial investment?

Apart from an infusion of God's value system, few of us will be satisfied with a modest life. Instead of seeking God, we will seek material gain to spend on ourselves or to hoard to our own hurt. We'll become self-satisfied (at least for a while) because material abundance tempts us to forget our dependence on God.

There's another serious problem with seeking wealth. Read Colossians 3:5-6.[133] What is equated with greed, and what are its consequences?

Warning! The pursuit of profit for the sake of wealth reveals our idolatry.[T33] And the consequence of idolatry—God's wrath—makes it imperative that we examine our attitudes about financial gains under the light of God's Word and the Holy Spirit.

SOURCES OF WEALTH

Suppose you wanted to get rich quick. Rank the following moneymaking methods according to their potential for rapid increase, beginning with "6" for the fastest method.

___ Stock market	___ Real estate
___ Sales	___ Personal labor
___ Gambling/lottery	___ Savings account

Proverbs 28:22 tells us that the one who wants to get rich quick has an evil eye. And eventually he's going to experience want. Do you think this is true? Why or why not?

HISTORY & CULTURE:[T33]

IDOLATRY—Idolatry was a deeply entrenched practice of the ancient Hebrews. We see the first mention of household idols in Genesis with the story of Jacob, whose wife Rachel stole her father's household gods.

When the children of Israel were in Egypt, they were introduced to a number of Egyptian deities, some of which they carried with them into the desert during their Exodus. When Moses was delayed on the mountain, the Israelites even made a golden calf to worship.

We tend to think of idol worship as simply bowing down before some image. But behind that small ritual lay hideous practices, including that of throwing children into the fire as an act of "worship." Idolatry was so offensive to God that He told the Israelites to annihilate all people and animals of certain descent and in certain regions of Canaan so they would not be tempted to "borrow" the religions of the people settled there. Israel failed to obey God, however, and fell into idolatry, just as God had predicted.

God finally "sold" the people of Israel into the hands of their enemies, who took them captive into Babylon territories for seventy years. This apparently broke the stronghold of idol worship for them because idolatry is not mentioned as a major theme after their return to Jerusalem from Babylonian captivity.

132 PROVERBS 11
28 He who trusts in his riches will fall, but the righteous will flourish like the green leaf.

133 COLOSSIANS 3
5-6 Consider the members of your earthly body as dead to immorality, impurity, passion, evil desire, and greed, which amounts to idolatry. For it is because of these things that the wrath of God will come.

134 PROVERBS 28
8 He who increases his wealth by interest and usury, gathers it for him who is gracious to the poor.

135 PROVERBS 20
23 Differing weights are an abomination to the LORD, and a false scale is not good.

136 DEUTERONOMY 23
19-20 You shall not charge interest to your countrymen: interest on money, food, or anything that may be loaned at interest. You may charge interest to a foreigner, but to your countryman you shall not charge interest, so that the LORD your God may bless you in all that you undertake in the land which you are about to enter to possess.

137 EZEKIEL 22
12 "You have taken interest and profits, and you have injured your neighbors for gain by oppression, and you have forgotten Me," declares the Lord GOD.

As you ranked the previous moneymaking methods, you probably noticed the relationship between those that offer the best potential for rapid or high investment returns and the increase in financial risk. Wealth gained by any means other than labor will likely dwindle—and will *surely* dwindle if gained in evil ways. What are some ways of making a profit that seem to meet with God's disapproval, as revealed in Proverbs 13:11,[126] 28:8,[134] and 20:23?[135]

We know that God is not pleased with profits made from evil enterprises, such as prostitution or theft, or by dishonesty, such as fraud or measuring out less than the amount our customer paid for. But what about interest and usury? Read God's Law from Deuteronomy 23:19-20[136] and Ezekiel 22:12.[137] When is interest sinful?

Ezekiel 22:12 uses a third Hebrew word, *tarbith,* for "profits." *Tarbith* means "interest or usury." It comes from the root word *rabah,* meaning "to grow large; to become great." Growing rich through usury is to exact high interest, making profit at the expense or misfortune of others. This receives strong rebuke by God. Those outside the Jewish community were not to be charged excessive interest, and those inside the community were not to be charged interest at all, especially if they were poor.

According to Deuteronomy 23:19-20,[137] what would the charging of interest cause the people to forfeit?

Read Job 20:4-23,26-29 from appendix A. As you read, note why the wicked man was unable to enjoy his wealth. What happened to his money when he died?

Why will the rich man's prosperity not endure, according to Job 20:21?

Paying high interest, or usury, rapidly depletes both the resources and the incentives needed for someone to continue producing. When that happens, there's nothing left for the rich to devour. Scripture warns us that lending at interest to our physical or spiritual family and charging exorbitant interest to anyone are ways of blocking God's blessings.

Read Psalm 15:1-2,5.[138] What are some characteristics of those who will please and abide with God?

If we expect to dwell with God, we must walk with integrity, work righteously, speak truth, and not lend money at interest if we decide to assist a friend. God wants us to profit by honest labor, not by moneymaking schemes that do not contribute positively to the larger community. Therefore, He tells us to work hard but not overwork, to build wealth with our labors, and to accumulate our assets slowly so that we may mature and increase in wisdom as we increase in riches.[T34]

BRINGING IT HOME

1. Do you think God's instructions to Israel concerning lending money at interest applies to us today? Why or why not? Is there any context wherein it might be appropriate to charge interest? If you've loaned money at interest, ask God to reveal whether you need to renegotiate the agreement to fit His Word.

2. Psalm 15 describes the transformed life through Christ. Examine the characteristics of the one who can abide with Christ (see appendix A). Do you see these traits in your life? Are you convicted by any of these traits? If so, write in the space below the area where God has convicted you. Confess this area to a trusted Christian friend and ask him or her to pray with you for God's transforming power. Also ask your prayer partner to hold you accountable.

POINT OF INTEREST:[T34]

WHEN ALL YOU CAN DO ISN'T ENOUGH—For several years I (Gail) owned and operated a small technical publications firm. Because our collective expertise was reporting on and proposing high-tech research, our primary market was federal labs and research organizations. Business was growing according to plan and, after three years, we landed a large contract. Our celebration was short-lived, however, when our work was suddenly canceled by a policy change within the Department of Energy.

I tried to save the business by working twice as many hours for half as much money. Needless to say, I eventually wrecked both my physical and my financial health.

Although I had prayed long and hard before starting the business, I don't pretend to comprehend God's purpose in the outcome. Nevertheless, I came to understand an important lesson: There is a point when all one can do will not be enough. I also learned that at the end of our own resources there's an incredible sweetness that comes from resting in the Lord.

SCRIPTURE MEDITATION

"For what will it profit a man, if he gains the whole world, and forfeits his soul? Or what will a man give in exchange for his soul?" (Matthew 16:26)

DAY 2

WORK AND PROSPERITY

[138]PSALM 15

1-2,5 O LORD, who may abide in Your tent? Who may dwell on Your holy hill? He who walks with integrity, and works righteousness, and speaks truth in his heart. . . . He does not put out his money at interest. . . . He who does these things will never be shaken.

[139]HAGGAI 1

6,9 "You have sown much, but harvest little; you eat, but there is not enough to be satisfied; you drink, but there is not enough to become drunk; you put on clothing, but no one is warm enough; and he who earns, earns wages to put into a purse with holes. . . . You look for much, but behold, it comes to little; when you bring it home, I blow it away. Why?" declares the LORD of hosts, "Because of My house which lies desolate, while each of you runs to his own house."

[140]DEUTERONOMY 6

10-12,15 When the LORD your God brings you into the land which he swore . . . to give you, great and splendid cities which you did not build, and houses full of all good things which you did not fill, and hewn cisterns which you did not dig, vineyards and olive trees which you did not plant, and you shall eat and are satisfied, then watch yourself, that you do not forget the LORD who brought you from the land of Egypt, out of the house of slavery. . . . For the LORD your God in the midst of you is a jealous God; otherwise the anger of the LORD your God will be kindled against you, and He will wipe you off the face of the earth.

We learned in yesterday's lesson that there is profit from labor. But how much direct effect does our labor have on our prosperity? Which one of the following do you think is most true?

__ Our prosperity will depend on how hard we work.
__ Our prosperity will depend on how smart we work.
__ Our prosperity will depend on how much we contribute to the well-being of society.
__ There is no causal relationship between our prosperity and any of the above.

Increasing one's labors may increase the *potential* for greater profits, but there's no real cause-and-effect relationship between work and prosperity. If hard work, smart work, or even socially valuable work always yielded prosperity, then farmers and bricklayers, college professors and scientists, or social workers and pastors would be filthy rich. But none of these professions is known for making one wealthy.

That work is not causally tied to prosperity is a rather shocking idea to most people—one that's a bit hard to accept. Let's look to Scripture to put this idea into perspective. Read Haggai 1:6,9.[139] What broke down the relationship between the people's work efforts and their prosperity?

According to the prophet Haggai, the people had begun to pursue their own interests instead of completing the mission God had given them to accomplish, namely, to rebuild the temple in Jerusalem. Though they were working hard, God was holding back their benefits because their priorities were out of order.

Let's examine another condition where the people's work efforts would not be productive. Read Deuteronomy 28:1-25,38-45 from appendix A. For what reason would God withhold profit from the people's labors, according to this passage?

God said, in essence, "If you choose to go your own way after entering into covenant with Me, then you can work all you want, but there will be no prosperity."

In these passages from Haggai and Deuteronomy we see examples of labor with no prosperity. God also gives prosperity with no labor. Read Deuteronomy 6:10-12,15.[140] How did the people gain the splendid cities, houses, vineyards, and so on, from Canaan?

God allowed the people of Israel to prosper by simply possessing their possessions. God's gifts were not earned but were the fulfillment of His promise to their fore-fathers—Abraham, Isaac, and Jacob.

The Old and New Covenant Blessings

The nation of Israel had made a covenant with God agreeing to His conditions of prosperity and blessings for their obedience and righteousness, as well as of poverty and cursings for disobedience and rebellion. This agreement did not apply, however, to those outside the covenant. Others could and did prosper in spite of their wickedness—sometimes even because of it!

The undeserving still prosper today. The greatest incomes often go to those who typically perform little manual labor, exert no superior intellect, and contribute little (or even negatively) to society, such as drug dealers, casino owners, or people in sports or entertainment industries.

Does something seem wrong with this picture? The psalmist struggled with this injustice as well.[T35] Read Psalm 73 from appendix A. Why was the psalmist upset (verses 3,10-12)?

What was he tempted to say (verse 13), and why didn't he say it (verse 15)?

What changed his perspective (verses 16-18,25-28)?

It is always tempting to think that prosperity should hinge on the honest labors of the righteous. Such human reasoning, however, will make us frustrated with God, for our eyes are on the temporal. This will cause us not only to

POINT OF INTEREST:[T35]

WHO GETS THE GOODS?— There are two elemental questions about Christianity that often cause people to stumble in their walk with God or in their attempts to understand God's ways. The first is "Why do bad things happen to good people?" The second is, "Why do evil people prosper?"

His answer to the first question was, simply, "There are no good people." At our best, we are fallen and in need of redemption. The psalmist did struggle with his understanding of God as he pondered the prosperity of the wicked (as recorded in Psalm 73, appendix A)—until, that is, he got an eternal perspective.

When we take a temporal look at God's distribution of goods and services, joys and pains, we can become frustrated with the Lord. But when we measure all assets from an eternal perspective, we see that the righteous poor have riches laid up in heaven that can't be compared with the riches allotted to those whose portion may be found in this life only.

When the Enemy brings this question to your mind, do as the psalmist did: change your perspective by remembering their end. Then pray for God to spare them from eternal death and bring them into His kingdom that they may share in *your* abundance.

[141]**JAMES 4**

13-16 Come now, you who say, "Today or tomorrow, we will . . . engage in business and make a profit." Yet you do not know what your life will be like tomorrow. You are just a vapor that appears for a little while and then vanishes away. Instead, you ought to say, "If the Lord wills, we will live and also do this or that." But as it is, you boast in your arrogance; all such boasting is evil.

[142]**HEBREWS 8**

1-2,6 Now the main point in what has been said is this: we have such a high priest, who has taken His seat at the right hand of the throne of the Majesty in the heavens, a minister in the sanctuary and in the true tabernacle, which the Lord pitched, not man. . . . Now He has obtained a more excellent ministry, by as much as He is also the mediator of a better covenant, which has been enacted on better promises.

stumble in our own walk with God, but also to become a stumbling block to others, especially those who are less mature in their understanding of God's ways. An eternal perspective will turn us around, however, for everything we might desire on earth is worthless compared to the surpassing value of the nearness of God, our portion.

Even when God Himself isn't withholding the profits from our labors, there are still a vast number of circumstances in our corrupt environment that can interfere with fruitfulness. Name some things that come to mind (perhaps some you've experienced yourself).

In spite of our best efforts, machines will break down, contracts will be lost, the economy will sag, unexpected expenses will crop up, weather will be uncooperative, our health will fail—the list is endless.

THE SPIRITUAL PRINCIPLE

How does it help us spiritually to know that there is no direct, causal relationship between how hard or how long we work and how prosperous we become?

In the face of financial losses, our first inclination is to double our efforts and try to out-earn the tough times. As long as we maintain the illusion that we can control our income by increasing our efforts, however, we will live our lives according to income rather than according to God's priorities. We will forget that more labor will demand more time and energy, both of which will have to come out of someone else's account—our time with God, our time with our families, our service to our churches and communities.

When we depend upon our own labors, we reveal our lack of faith and trust in God as our only real source of provision. Instead of doubling our work efforts, then, we should double our time in prayer. Read James 4:13-16.[141] What does James say is the right approach to making a profit?

As ambassadors for His kingdom, we must seek God's leading, even in our work efforts.

We cannot leave today's study without looking at the relationship between God's covenant with Israel and the New Covenant Christ makes with us when we come to Him for salvation, for these are not the same.

Read Hebrews 8:1-2,6.[142] Which is better: the Old Covenant or the New Covenant? Why?

The children of Israel were promised abundance in the fruit of the vine by keeping covenant. Under the New Covenant, the relationship between righteousness and prosperity is not material but spiritual. God promises that, as we keep His covenant, we will abound in the fruit of the Spirit through our relationship to Him. It is to our joy and to God's glory that we prosper under that covenant, even as our soul prospers (3 John 1:2).

BRINGING IT HOME

1. Material blessings are not tied to our covenant relationship with Christ. Nevertheless, God's financial principles are still relevant and should be examined in the light of our work lives. Go back over those principles listed in today's study. List those that may be a stumbling block to you and ask God to help you adjust your attitudes or spending habits to better reflect His glory in your Christian walk.

SCRIPTURE MEDITATION

"But store up for yourselves treasures in heaven, where neither moth nor rust destroys, and where thieves do not break in or steal; for where your treasure is, there your heart will be also."
(Ecclesiastes 9:11)

DAY 3

WORK AND PROVISION

Yesterday we learned that there is no real cause-and-effect relationship between work and prosperity. But what about provision?

Picture yourself conducting a random survey on a busy street where you're asking men and women, "Why do you go to work?" The overwhelming majority would give an answer something like, "To make money." That is, they work for a paycheck to pay for their living expenses. Most likely, however, a number of those people in your survey would be from two-income households where one person's income would cover their needs. Also, a few could be independently wealthy and still others might just love what they do. What percentage of the work force would you think actually goes to work for some reason *other* than provision?

This was a tricky question—the answer is 100 percent. Most people think they go to work to meet their needs, of course, but no person's provision really comes from working. Read Psalms 127:2[143] and 147:8-9.[144] How are needs supplied? When?

God provides for all of His creation. God gifted people with skills and gave them work as a means of expressing their talents. God also established a system by which people's labors would serve as a vehicle for distributing God's provisions. But a vehicle is not the same as a source any more than a conveyor belt is the same as the item it transports. Read Matthew 6:24,31-33.[145] What does this passage tell us *not* to do?

In Matthew 6, Jesus says four times not to be worried or anxious. Literally, don't even think about it. God provides even for the animals who do no work at all. You are not solely responsible for meeting your own needs, but you

---

[143]**PSALM 127**

2 It is vain for you to rise up early, to retire late, to eat the bread of painful labors; for He gives to His beloved even in his sleep.

[144]**PSALM 147**

8-9 [The Lord] provides rain for the earth, . . . makes grass to grow on the mountains . . . gives to the beast its food.

[145]**MATTHEW 6**

24,31-33 "No one can serve two masters. . . . You cannot serve God and wealth. . . . Do not worry then, saying, 'What will we eat?' or 'What will we drink?' or 'What will we wear for clothing?' . . . For your heavenly Father knows that you need all these things. But seek first His kingdom and His righteousness, and all these things will be added to you."

[146]**GENESIS 2**

7-9 The LORD God formed man . . . ; and man became a living being. The LORD God planted a garden . . . ; and there He placed the man whom He had formed. Out of the ground the LORD God caused to grow every tree that is . . . good for food.

[147]**PSALM 146**

6-7 [The Lord] made heaven and earth, the sea and all that is in them; . . . keeps faith forever; . . . gives food to the hungry.

are solely responsible for obeying God's directive to work.

Read Genesis 2:7-9[146] and Psalm 146:6-7.[147] When did God first make provision for people? Why would our heavenly Father be the only One who could really satisfy our needs?

Our heavenly Father made us. He knows what we need better than we do, and He alone can satisfy us. If He withholds any good thing, it will be to drive us to Himself. Often it is through our discovery of our own inadequacies that we become more spiritually receptive, perhaps even receiving correction of our wrong ideas of self-sufficiency.[T36]

SEEING GOD AS PROVIDER

Read Malachi 3:8-10.[148] What was the relationship between giving and provision?

What was the spiritual problem identified in these three verses?

What difference might it make in the way you approach your work if you truly believed that God, not your work, was your source of provision? How, for example, might it affect your stress level?

If we could grasp the truth that God is our source of provision, then we would be relieved of a tremendous amount of stress in the workplace. For example, we would eliminate concerns about losing our jobs and be relieved of pressures to get promoted. We wouldn't be concerned about economic reversals or corporate downsizing or our jobs becoming obsolete. We'd also probably develop a more-balanced relationship among work, family, leisure, and worship.

How might seeing God as our source of provision affect our relationships with our coworkers or clients?

POINT OF INTEREST:[T36]

TEMPTED TO BOAST—How many people do you know who have had much of this world's wealth and then lost it all over a short period of time? If they've defined their significance and success on things that turned out to be hollow in the long run, then their very identity may have crumbled.

The source of significance is found in Jeremiah 9: "Thus says the LORD, 'Let not a wise man boast of his wisdom, and let not the mighty man boast of his might, let not a rich man boast of his riches; but let him who boasts boast of this, that he understands and knows Me, that I am the LORD who exercises lovingkindness, justice and righteousness on earth" (verses 23-24).

Right away we've eliminated three basic things—wealth, wisdom, and power—that people pursue for significance in our culture.

Wealth, wisdom, and power are not impressive. They are shallow in comparison to what God offers. People believe they are important to the degree that they excel in one or more of these things. They'll go for the gold, but they'll take the silver or bronze (beauty or talent or power). But however we define success, it will be transient and hollow unless it is connected to kingdom purposes.

[148]MALACHI 3

8-10 "Will a man rob God? Yet you are robbing Me! But you say, 'How have we robbed You?' In tithes and offerings. You are cursed with a curse, for you are robbing Me, the whole nation of you! Bring the whole tithe into the storehouse, so that there may be food in My house, and test Me now in this," says the LORD of hosts, "if I will not open for you the windows of heaven, and pour out for you a blessing until it overflows."

[149]COLOSSIANS 3

22-24 Slaves, in all things obey those who are your masters . . . with sincerity of heart, fearing the Lord. . . . Do your work heartily, as for the Lord rather than for men, knowing that from the Lord you will receive the reward of the inheritance. It is the Lord Christ whom you serve.

[150]ECCLESIASTES 9

10 Whatever your hand finds to do, do it with all your might.

[151]ECCLESIASTES 9

11 I again saw under the sun that the race is not to the swift and the battle is not to the warriors, and neither is bread to the wise nor wealth to the discerning nor favor to men of ability; for time and chance overtake them all.

When we see work as our source of provision, we tend to play the game like everyone else does. We're competitive with our coworkers. We're tempted to compromise our character and integrity in the face of financial or emotional setbacks. We even use rather than serve our clients.

The minute we start to think of our work as our *source* of provision rather than our *vehicle* of provision, we'll begin to embrace a manipulative attitude toward others. We'll start to see them as a means by which we fulfill our needs and make a living. Rather than trying to minister to them, we'll be trying to use them.

Do you think seeing God as your source of provision could affect your productivity? If so, negatively or positively?

Seeing God as our source of provision does not mean we just sit back and passively wait for our money to fall from heaven. That would be a total misunderstanding, one that would make us lazy. Read Colossians 3:22-24[149] and Ecclesiastes 9:10.[150] How are we to work? Check all the statements below that are true, based on these verses.

____ We should obey our bosses outwardly and keep our grumbling to ourselves.

____ We should obey our bosses with a willing heart.

____ We should work hard with the motivation of serving our bosses.

____ We should work hard with the motivation of serving the Lord.

____ We should work as hard as we can.

____ We should work only as hard as necessary to get by.

We are still commanded to work heartily—with all our might—but for different reasons. Instead of working for provision, we work to please God. We keep looking to God for the results, even when we don't know what He's going to do. From an earthly point of view, we'll be operating in a major risk-taking mode, for God's ways are always counter-cultural. This can be a little frightening in the beginning, until we learn to trust in God's promises.

Although it's a solid eternal investment, working as unto the Lord may not result in earthly gain. Why might this be true?

As we've seen in Scripture, God may withhold prosperity from us because of our spiritual needs or disobedience. Read Ecclesiastes 9:11.[151] What is another reason we might not be prosperous in our work efforts?

All the preparation in the world won't matter if there are no opportunities or market. You may be the best at what you do and you may work the hardest and you may be the fastest. But ability alone matters not at all; opportunity and timing also have to converge.

While we really can't control our income levels, we can put our hope in God's character and in His promise for provision. And when we do, we will free up our work arena to be a context for the expression of the life of Christ in a marketplace community.[T37]

BRINGING IT HOME

1. Many people pursue rewards of labor that have no eternal value. In what ways could you pursue Christ in your work arena as an end in itself and not for earthly awards?

2. Think about how the Lord has provided for you in ways that did not come through your work. For example, how were you provided for when you were a helpless baby and young child? How were your education or training opportunities provided? Where did you get your spouse or children? List some of the blessings you have that aren't related to your own work efforts. Be sure to give God thanks and praise for these immeasurable gifts.

CROSS-REFERENCES:[T37]

WISDOM AND WEALTH—The Bible has a lot to say about how we use our money. The following exercise will provide a good overview of God's instructions from Psalms and Proverbs. Divide a sheet of paper into two columns, labeling one column "Blessings" and the other column "Warnings." As you look up each of the following Scriptures, briefly summarize the passage and write what you learn in the appropriate column. Also look up and note a few of the cross-references that are listed in these verses. (Cross-reference only those verses that contain the words "wealth" or "riches.") When you are finished, spend some time reflecting on the relationship between God's commandments and your own attitude about riches and wealth.

Proverbs: 3:9-10; 11:28; 13:22; 15:6; 22:4; 23:4-5; 27:23-24; 28:8; 28:22

Psalms: 49:5-12; 49:16-20; 52:1-7; 62:10; 112:1-3

SCRIPTURE MEDITATION

The steps of a man are established by the LORD; and He delights in his way. When he falls, he shall not be hurled headlong; because the LORD is the One who holds his hand. I have been young and now I am old, yet I have not seen the righteous forsaken or his descendants begging bread. All day long he is gracious and lends, and his descendants are a blessing. (Psalm 37:23-26)

DAY 4

WORK AND WAGES

As we learned earlier, our labors are the source neither of our prosperity nor our provision. God created and continues to sustain an abundance of natural resources. He gifts each of us with a unique skill set and provides us with ways to learn and grow. He also gives us productive opportunities and confirms and blesses (or withholds his confirmation and blessing from) the work of our hands. He is our provider; we need not fear.[T38]

Nevertheless, God has ordained work as the mechanism or vehicle through which He supplies our needs. That is, as we use our skills toward shaping the earth's resources into something useful for the human race, we normally experience material increase through diligent labors.

Most of us labor collectively, and for our efforts we receive a portion of the total profits in the form of fees, royalties, tips, salaries, or wages. Scripture has a lot to say about our paying for another's labors. Read Leviticus 19:13[152] and Deuteronomy 24:14-15.[153] According to these verses, when should you pay someone who is working for you?

People who need their money right away are looked down upon in our culture. But according to Scripture, the error rests with those who do not immediately pay. Read Malachi 3:5[154] and James 5:1,4-5.[155] What are some of the consequences of neglecting to fairly pay those you hire or neglecting to pay them promptly?

Whether we have hired people to help us make a profit or to help us with a household chore, Scripture tells us to pay hired laborers at the appointed time—even at the end of their day's work if they need it. Failure to pay a person his or her full earned wages at the proper time puts us under God's judgment, for we are not only violating the rights and needs of another person but we are thwarting the mechanism God has put in place for that person's provision.

---

[152]**LEVITICUS 19**

13 The wages of a hired man are not to remain with you all night until morning.

[153]**DEUTERONOMY 24**

14-15 You shall not oppress a hired servant who is poor and needy. . . . You shall give him his wages on his day before the sun sets, for he is poor and sets his heart on it; so that he may not cry against you to the LORD and it become sin in you.

[154]**MALACHI 3**

5 "I will draw near to you for judgment; and I will be a swift witness . . . against the adulterers and against those who swear falsely, and against those who oppress the wage earner in his wages, the widow and the orphan, and those who turn aside the alien and do not fear Me," says the LORD of hosts.

[155]**JAMES 5**

1,4-5 Come now, you rich, weep and howl for your miseries which are coming upon you. . . . Behold, the pay of the laborers who mowed your fields, and which has been withheld by you, cries out against you; and the outcry of those who did the harvesting has reached the ears of the Lord of Sabaoth. You have lived luxuriously on the earth and led a life of wanton pleasure; you have fattened your hearts in a day of slaughter.

[156]**COLOSSIANS 3 & 4**

3:25 He who does wrong will receive the consequences of the wrong which he has done, and that without partiality.
4:1 Masters, grant to your slaves justice and fairness, knowing that you too have a Master in heaven.

God will see to it that there is a payday someday, both for those who labor and for those who take advantage of or devalue the labors of others, no matter who they are. Read Colossians 3:25 and 4:1.[156] What is the obligation of masters, and what are the consequences of their treating badly those who are under their care?

Read Exodus 3:21-22.[157] How were both Egypt and the children of Israel compensated for years of wrongful slavery?

God has always had a principle of fair treatment of those we employ, whether as slaves or as hirelings. Egypt violated that principle. If you read the entire account of God's retribution on the Egyptians (Exodus 11–12), you'll see a severe redistribution of the very wealth that Egypt had built on the backs of the Hebrews. Egypt was left impoverished; the Israelites walked away with "back pay."

The importance of not taking advantage of someone else's labors or livelihood was also modeled by Jesus. Read Luke 5:1-7,11 from appendix A. What do you see in this passage that illustrates compensation for Peter's assistance?

Peter fished for a living. He and his crew had worked hard all night, but there was no yield for their labors. No doubt Peter was tired and discouraged, and he was certainly busy washing those heavy nets. Suppose you had been Peter. How might you have reacted to the Lord's request?

Because Peter was a commercial fisherman, his boat was probably thirty feet long or more. Launching and anchoring it was no minor chore. As the true owner of everything, the Son of God had every right to leave without so much as a "thank you." Instead, He repaid Peter with an abundant catch. Most likely, those fish were worth far more than a fair market price for the short use of Peter's boat.

What did Peter and the others do after they got the fish-laden boats to shore?

POINT OF INTEREST:[T38]

WORRY—Worry is always directed at the future. One reason we look for security in our jobs is that we experience personal frustration, anxiety, uncertainty, and insecurity about what the future holds. In His Sermon on the Mount, Jesus said that there would always be enough present-day difficulties and that we need not borrow speculative burdens from the future. The load is too great to bear. God meters life to us one day at a time, and each day brings its own opportunities and challenges. We need all of our mental energies to deal with the concerns of each day—concerns that keep us spiritually, mentally, and emotionally engaged.

Worry won't add an inch to our height, but it can bend our shoulders under its weight. Worry can't extend our lives, but it can shorten them. We can become pulled apart by the multiplicity of concerns that can consume our thinking, even our sleeping.

Worry is not just *un*productive, it's *counter*productive. Worry won't give us greater control, but it will take away the control we have over our present circumstances. And living in the present is the closest we come to experiencing an eternal "now."

Jesus taught us not to be anxious or worry about the future because He has the future under control; He is our provider. "Take . . . no thought for the morrow," He says. "Sufficient unto the day is the evil thereof" (Matthew 6:34, KJV).

[157] EXODUS 3

21-22 [God said to Moses,] "I will grant this people favor in the sight of the Egyptians; and it shall be that when you go, you will not go empty-handed. But every woman shall ask of her neighbor . . . articles of silver and articles of gold, and clothing; and you will put them on your sons and daughters. Thus you will plunder the Egyptians."

[158] MATTHEW 19

28-29 Jesus said to them, "Truly I say to you, that you who have followed Me . . . will sit upon twelve thrones, judging the twelve tribes of Israel. And everyone who has left houses or brothers or sisters or father or mother or children or farms for My name's sake, will receive many times as much, and will inherit eternal life."

[159] 1 TIMOTHY 5

17-18 The elders who rule well are to be considered worthy of double honor, especially those who work hard at preaching and teaching. For the Scripture says, "YOU SHALL NOT MUZZLE THE OX WHILE HE IS THRESHING," and "The laborer is worthy of his wages."

[160] RUTH 2

11-12 Boaz replied to her, ". . . May the LORD reward your work, and your wages be full from the LORD, the God of Israel, under whose wings you have come to seek refuge."

Check one.

___ Carted the fish to the nearest market

___ Left the catch of fish to rot

___ Left the fishing industry to follow Jesus

___ Scripture doesn't say

Scripture leaves us wondering what became of that great catch of fish. All we know is that Peter, James, and John recognized something far more valuable, for they left catch, boat, and all to follow Jesus.

Jesus began to train these fishermen to catch others with the hook of the gospel. As Peter was being discipled, he asked Jesus a question that revealed his spiritual immaturity: "Behold, we have left everything and followed You; what then will there be for us?" (Matthew 19:27).

Again, we might expect Jesus to be indignant. After all, being a comrade of the One who created him should have been reward enough for Peter. But read Jesus' answer from Matthew 19:28-29.[158] What would be the disciples' reward for leaving everything and following Jesus?

Jesus' answer illustrates God's principle of generous rewards for our labors, even in the spiritual realm.

Now read Matthew 20:1-16 from appendix A. Does the landowner in this passage strike you as fair or unfair? Why?

What is the landowner's reasoning? Does he or does he not have a valid point?

There are at least two views of justice, called distributive and retributive. Distributive justice in this case would say that those who worked longer should make more money. But retributive justice (on which our laws are based) recognizes that the landowner has not cheated anyone out of a fair day's wage (a denarius). He gave everyone their due, and out of his generosity gave some more than their due. The landowner (who represents Jesus) kept his bargain but was under no obligation to distribute his extra giving according to works.

Read 1 Timothy 5:17-18[159] and Ruth 2:11-12.[160] According to these Scriptures and others in today's study, does God pay us fairly for our labors in His kingdom? Support your answer.

Scripture assures us that we will receive, at minimum, fair wages for our work, both on earth and as an eternal reward. But God is free to give us even more than we've earned, and He can distribute excess gifts as He pleases.

If we calculate compensation according to the value of our labor, then we would all be impoverished. Yet God's provisions exceed all that we could ask or think (Ephesians 3:20). If we would reflect Christ, then, we too must freely and generously reward those whose labors we employ.[T39]

BRINGING IT HOME

1. If you are in a position to employ other people directly, how do you (or your company) determine the salaries of those under your care? By asking (a) "How much can I (we) pay them and still earn a reasonable profit margin?" or (b) "How little can we pay them without losing them to competitors?" If (b), what are you going to do to fix the problem?

2. Think of those who perform services for you personally. How fairly do you pay the one who mows your lawn or cleans your house? How generous are you with tips? Do you ask people to lower their reasonable fees to accommodate your finances? Mentally trade places with the person you are employing. How would you want to be treated? If you have a genuine need (such as a car repair or medical attention) and cannot afford to pay a fair and just wage for those services, ask God to supply the money you need so that you can honor Him in the area of wages.

3. There is no objective basis nor biblical support for valuing one person's skill over another's. Ask God to remove the culture's value system from your thinking and to give you His perspective. Follow through by paying fair wages to those who provide personal or professional services to you.

POINT OF INTEREST:[T39]

ALL WORK IS EQUALLY HONORABLE—Most people in our culture place mental work on a higher plane than manual labor (at least until they need a plumber). Scripture, however, always places value and honor on all honest labors. This doesn't mean, of course, that we don't have abilities and capabilities that differ widely. We are to recognize that some will be more skillful in some areas, others will have greater dexterity, and still others will have greater intellectual capacity.

Instead of trying to force some kind of nonsensical egalitarianism (as if that would be a great leveler of humankind), we should be celebrating these differences and working to elevate manual laborers to the dignity that their occupations deserve.

SCRIPTURE MEDITATION

Who at any time serves as a soldier at his own expense? Who plants a vineyard and does not eat the fruit of it? Or who tends a flock and does not use the milk of the flock? . . . For it is written in the Law of Moses, "YOU SHALL NOT MUZZLE THE OX WHILE HE IS THRESHING." God is not concerned about oxen, is He? Or is He speaking altogether for our sake? Yes, for our sake it was written, because the plowman ought to plow in hope, and the thresher to thresh in hope of sharing the crops. If we sowed spiritual things in you, is it too much if we should reap material things from you?"
(1 Corinthians 9:7,9-11)

DAY 5

WORK AND ABUNDANCE

As we look around us, it's obvious that God has allowed some to accumulate considerable wealth while others attain only minimal subsistence. There are many reasons, or combinations of reasons, that this may be true.[T40]

First, God gives us principles that, if followed, are more likely to result in the accumulation of wealth. Read Psalm 37:11[161] and Proverbs 28:19-20,[162] 3:9-10,[163] 11:18,[164] 15:6,[165] and 22:4.[166] What are some principles that contribute to wealth building, according to these verses?

What are some principles of losing wealth or income, according to these same verses as well as Haggai 1:6,9,[139] Jeremiah 17:11,[167] and Proverbs 28:8?[134]

There are many other references to God's conditions for accruing wealth, but among those we've noted in this unit are working diligently; being humble, righteous, and faithful; fearing the Lord and honoring Him in our giving; being obedient; and paying fair wages to those who work for us.

Likewise we've learned ways to avoid losing wealth or income by not following empty pursuits; not trying to get rich quick; not being deceptive, fraudulent, or unjust in our business dealings; not wrongly charging interest or usury; not neglecting God's house; and not oppressing the poor.

If someone met all the criteria in the above paragraphs, do you think that person would automatically become wealthy? Why or why not?

For those of us in the kingdom of God, the criteria for accumulating wealth present something of a dilemma. Even if we did the "do's" and avoided the "don'ts," we would still be disqualified for wealth by the very desire for it. God's words on financial issues are not to be taken as a list of attributes for obtaining riches. They are, instead, the

[161]**PSALM 37**
11 The humble will inherit the land and will delight themselves in abundant prosperity.

[162]**PROVERBS 28**
19-20 He who tills his land will have plenty of food, but he who follows empty pursuits will have poverty in plenty. A faithful man will abound with blessings, but he who makes haste to be rich will not go unpunished.

[163]**PROVERBS 3**
9-10 Honor the LORD from your wealth, and from the first of all your produce; so your barns will be filled with plenty, and your vats will overflow with new wine.

[164]**PROVERBS 11**
18 The wicked earns deceptive wages, but he who sows righteousness gets a true reward.

[165]**PROVERBS 15**
6 Great wealth is in the house of the righteous, but trouble is in the income of the wicked.

[166]**PROVERBS 22**
4 The reward of humility and the fear of the LORD are riches, honor and life.

[167]**JEREMIAH 17**
11 He who makes a fortune, but unjustly; in the midst of his days it will forsake him, and in the end he will be a fool.

[168]**ECCLESIASTES 5**
19 For every man to whom God has given riches and wealth, He has also empowered him to eat from them and to receive his reward and rejoice in his labor; this is the gift of God.

[169]**PROVERBS 10**
22 It is the blessing of the LORD that makes rich, and He adds no sorrow to it.

attributes that naturally flow out of a deep love for the Father and a desire to serve Him with all that comes into our possession. God can and does allow both Christians and non-Christians to accumulate wealth, but only the spiritually mature will be able to handle an abundance in ways that please God and advance His kingdom.

Compare Ecclesiastes 5:19[168] and Proverbs 10:22[169] with Ecclesiastes 4:8.[170] In the spaces following, list indicators of spiritual maturity and spiritual immaturity (or unbelief) relating to material abundance, according to these verses.

Mature Attitudes About Abundance

-

-

-

Immature Attitudes About Abundance

-

-

-

Spiritually mature Christians tend to enjoy their work and view the workplace as their mission field. They rejoice as much over their daily provision as they do over their abundance. Any wealth they happen to accumulate is not a burden to them, for they hold it openhandedly before the Lord. Regardless of their circumstances, they have learned the same important secret Paul spoke of in Philippians 4:11-13.[171] What is it?

How did Paul remain content, even in adversity?

[170]**ECCLESIASTES 4**

8 There was a certain man without a dependent, . . . yet there was no end to all his labor. Indeed, his eyes were not satisfied with riches. . . . This too is vanity.

[171]**PHILIPPIANS 4**

11-13 I have learned to be content in whatever circumstances I am. I know how to get along with humble means, and I also know how to live in prosperity; . . . I have learned the secret of being filled and going hungry. . . . I can do all things through Him who strengthens me.

[172]**1 TIMOTHY 6**

17-19 Instruct those who are rich in this present world not to be conceited or to fix their hope on the uncertainty of riches, but on God, who richly supplies us with all things to enjoy. Instruct them to do good, to be rich in good works, to be generous and ready to share, storing up for themselves the treasure of a good foundation for the future, so that they may take hold of that which is life indeed.

[173]**HEBREWS 11**

24-26 By faith Moses . . . [chose] rather to endure ill-treatment with the people of God, than to enjoy the passing pleasures of sin; considering the reproach of Christ greater riches than the treasures of Egypt; for he was looking to the reward.

Like Paul, mature Christians draw both contentment and strength from their relationship with the Creator God. Circumstances fade in the light of the love of God and in the power of His Spirit. The unbeliever (and even the spiritually immature), on the other hand, rarely remain content—even with prosperity. They are often dissatisfied with their work. Typically, they'll have an insatiable appetite for material gain, worry excessively about losing possessions, and spend their wealth on themselves. Unbelievers cannot comprehend spiritual contentment.

From the contrast in attitudes, it stands to reason that those who have not learned the secret of contentment would be drawn to those who have. What a marvelous opportunity for introducing the gospel in the workplace![T41]

STEWARDSHIP

As we've mentioned earlier, the Old Covenant promised material abundance to the covenant keeper. God has given us a new and better covenant with better promises, namely, promises of spiritual abundance for the covenant keeper. If material wealth is not promised to the believer, then why might God give an abundance to the Christian today? Read 1 Timothy 6:17-19[172] and Hebrews 11:24-26[173] before you answer.

On what should the rich focus their hopes?

Scripture instructs those with abundance to use their wealth in ways that honor God, namely, by financing good works, generously sharing with the less fortunate, and storing up treasures in heaven. We must not conclude from these Scriptures that the wealthy Christian cannot rightly enjoy any of the benefits of wealth. We also must not conclude that the way into heaven is through investing our time, talent, and treasure in the work of the kingdom. We know from the full counsel of God that the only way to heaven is through pardon of our sin debt by the reconciling work of Jesus at Calvary. We must be born again! Evidence of our rebirth, however, will be a change from a temporal perspective to an eternal perspective. When our perspective changes, so will our spending habits.

BRINGING IT HOME

1. If you became content with what you have, how would that attitude change the following situations:

   a. How you interact with people in business

   b. How you make spending choices

   c. How you deal with stress

   What will you do this week to begin improving in each of these areas?

2. Matthew 25:13-30 encourages us in the wise use of our resources—time, talent, and treasures—for we will be held accountable before the Lord for what we've done with each of these things. Rate yourself from 1 (poor) to 10 (excellent) in each of these categories.

   a. Use of time _____

   b. Use of talents _____

   c. Use of treasures _____

   Spend some time before the Lord before you answer. Ask God to show you how to increase your efficiency in the use of each of these resources.

CONTENTMENT—I (Gail) have had the great privilege of sharing the gospel with a coworker, Roy, and then watching him take off like a rocket in his walk with the Lord. Since his conversion, he has suffered through many trials, some extremely difficult. Most recently, he lost his job as a result of downsizing, just two years before he was eligible for full retirement benefits.

Most people would have been undone by the troubles that Roy and his wife, Shirley, have experienced. Yet in everything, their joy remains undiminished. Roy was actually excited about his termination because, as he said, "It meant I got to work full-time for God two years earlier than I'd planned."

Roy's attitude at work drew many hurting people to him, for the world is hungry for answers on how to handle adversity. We can all learn something from this kind of contentment. It is greatly encouraging to see someone walking in such faith and dependence on God. How are you handling adversity?

SCRIPTURE MEDITATION

I count all things to be loss in view of the surpassing value of knowing Christ Jesus my Lord, for whom I have suffered the loss of all things, and count them but rubbish so that I may gain Christ. (Philippians 3:8)

SHARING THE JOURNEY

To the leader: As an option, you might want to make play money totaling $10 million and give it to group members by turns for disbursement in the final activity.

1. Earning profit through honest labor is perfectly legitimate. It's only when we are obsessed with profit that it becomes an occasion for sin. So, for example, we should not get caught up in get-rich-quick schemes. Nor should we charge excessive interest.

   • What do the Hebrew words *yaal* and *mothar* teach us about the nature of profit?

   • What effects can greed have on one's spiritual life? Cite real-life examples if you can.

   • A friend of yours has just invited you to join him in a high-risk investment that would require most of your savings. What are some things you should consider before responding?

   • If we were to take the Old Testament laws about charging interest and apply them today, what are some ways we might do that?

2. Working harder or longer will not necessarily make us more prosperous. Circumstances or even God Himself may prevent us from making as much money as we think we deserve. But if we are faithful to our covenant with God, we can always count on spiritual prosperity, and that's far more important.

   • What reasons might God have for withholding prosperity from Christians today?

   • Name things that might prevent people from accumulating wealth even though they have worked hard. For each of these, identify how it is directly or indirectly related to sin.

   • On page 80 we read that, when hard times hit, we should not double our work efforts but should double our time in prayer. What's your reaction to that approach?

   • Name some ways that God has blessed you with spiritual prosperity.

3. It may seem that it's our jobs that provide for our needs, but on a deeper level, it's really God who provides all good things. Consequently, our motivation in working should not be to provide for ourselves but to please God.

   • How much stress does your work give you? How much, if any, of that stress might be relieved if you focused on God as your provider?

   • What are some practical ways that your approach to work might change if you were to constantly recognize God—and not your work—as the true source of your provision?

4. Scripture consistently teaches that employers must treat their workers fairly. This includes paying them promptly and adequately. God is far more gracious to us than we deserve, and we should display a similar generosity to others.

   • On a sheet of paper, list the names of all the people whose work you pay for (employees, baby-sitters, lawn care workers, and so on). Then, for each one, think through these questions: Are you paying them as little as you can get by with, or are you paying them as much as their work is worth? Are you paying them within an accepted time frame—or even sooner, if they have a need for it?

   • If a Christian wanted to be more fair in paying others, how could he or she determine what a reasonable amount and schedule for payment would be?

5. Christians are not promised material wealth, but when God chooses to bestow that blessing upon them, they are responsible to handle their abundance in ways that honor God and advance His kingdom. It takes spiritual maturity to handle wealth wisely.

   • Have you ever known a believer who had considerable wealth and handled it in a godly way? Tell about that person.

   • It is said that spiritually mature Christians don't care whether they are rich or poor, and that they hold their wealth with open hands before the Lord. Would you say that these characteristics apply to you? If not, share ideas with each other about how to grow in this area.

   • Let's say that you just inherited $10 million and that your primary goal in life is to maximize your "treasures in heaven." What will you do with the money? (And here's the kicker: What's stopping you from doing some of those things right now?)

Close your session with prayer for the Lord's help as group members try to handle their finances in more godly ways. Express gratitude to God for blessing us far above what we deserve.

INTRODUCTION TO UNIT 5
WORK AND CHARACTER

Destination: To understand how our character is reflected in our work habits.

Our national character is an enigma. On the one hand, we are a generous people. America has, by far, more philanthropists than any other country in the world. Our level of giving, in fact, is unique among the countries in this world. When Americans become extremely rich, many give away huge sums of money to be used for the public good. In fact, much of what the citizenry enjoys today (libraries, parks, museums, universities, and so on) was made available to us through the contributions of wealthy philanthropists, such as Carnegie and Rockefeller, as well as middle-class and even poor Americans who have given liberally and sacrificially for some common good.

But even in America, generous givers are more the exception than the rule. That is, the number of people who give generously is significantly smaller than the number of those who either don't give at all or else give sparingly in comparison to their resources. And far too many Americans pursue riches not only at the expense of the common good but also at the expense of their ethical moorings and their personal relationships.

What is at stake for the majority of Americans is an erosion of character in the workplace, because it's there that choices are most often presented between income and ethics, between workaholism and a balanced lifestyle. In his book *Work, Play, and Worship in a Leisure-Oriented Society*, Gordon Dahl wrote, "Most middle-class Americans tend to worship their work, work at their play, and play at their worship. As a result, their meanings and values are distorted. Their relationships disintegrate faster than they can keep them in repair, and their life-styles resemble a cast of characters in search of a plot."

In unit 5 we look at some common issues relating to workplace decisions that can distort our values and disrupt our relationships. The studies in this unit, however, are designed to help us reorient our scrambled priorities. Through God's Word we can establish healthy life habits so that we might learn to work at our work, play at our play, and worship at our worship. Ask God to give you insight as you examine yourself in the light of His Word.

[174]**PROVERBS 12**
17 He who speaks truth [emunah] tells what is right.

[175]**PROVERBS 28**
20 A faithful [emunah] man will abound with blessings.

[176]**ISAIAH 33**
6 [Jesus] will be the stability [emunah] of your times, a wealth of salvation, wisdom and knowledge.

[177]**ISAIAH 59**
4 No one pleads honestly [emunah]. They trust in confusion and speak lies.

[178]**1 TIMOTHY 1**
15 It is a trustworthy [pistos] statement, deserving full acceptance, that Christ Jesus came into the world to save sinners.

[179]**ROMANS 6**
17-18 Though you were slaves of sin, you became obedient from the heart to that form of teaching to which you were committed, and having been freed from sin, you became slaves of righteousness.

[180]**PHILIPPIANS 2**
5-8 Have this attitude in yourselves which was also in Christ Jesus, who, although He existed in the form of God, did not regard equality with God a thing to be grasped, but emptied Himself, taking the form of a bond-servant, and being made in the likeness of men. Being found in appearance as a man, He humbled Himself by becoming obedient to the point of death, even death on a cross.

DAY 1

ATTRIBUTES OF GOD'S EMPLOYEES

Let's take a baseline reading of what it means to be a good employee.[T42] Imagine you owned a company (perhaps you actually do). List in their order of importance the top five attributes you would look for in an employee (not including being a Christian).

1.

2.

3.

4.

5.

How many of these relate to character? _____

Whether or not they realize it, the greatest need of all employers is employees who are faithful. Does "faithfulness" seem out of place in the context of work? How is this term normally used?

Outside the spiritual realm, the attribute of faithfulness tends to be used only in the context of marital or dating relationships. But the biblical concept of faithfulness encompasses most of the attributes of good character—a full range of morals and ethics that all employers want in an employee.

There are several Hebrew words for "faithfulness," each of which is derived from the root word *aman,* meaning "to confirm or support." *Aman* speaks of "that which has been established or verified" or "that which has been tested and found reliable, trustworthy, and lasting."

Of the various Hebrew words derived from the root word *aman,* the one that relates most specifically to personal character is *emunah.* Note how this word is used in Proverbs 12:17[174] and 28:20,[175] as well as Isaiah 33:6[176] and 59:4.[177] Summarize the attributes that are encompassed in this Hebrew word, according to the way *emunah* is translated.

In addition to "faithfulness," the Hebrew *emunah* is translated in various texts as "steadfastness," "fidelity," "honesty," "responsibility," "stability," and "truth." Its closest parallel word in Greek is *pistos*. *Pistos* means the same as *emunah* but includes the idea of being fully persuaded and totally confident in that which has been tested and found to be reliable, trustworthy, steadfast, and true. What central theme, then, do you think *pistos* often refers to in the New Testament?

Pistos is the word used in Scripture to describe the type of saving faith that the true believer has in Jesus Christ. It is the confidence and trust in God that belongs to those who have been born again.

Read 1 Timothy 1:15.[178] What is the reliable statement noted in this verse?

This short verse tells us three important points of Christian doctrine that are further illustrated in the following verses. Write these points in the spaces provided.

1. All have sinned and fall short of the glory of God. (Romans 3:23)

2. He who believes in the Son has eternal life; but he who does not obey the Son will not see life, but the wrath of God abides on him. (John 3:36)

3. Jesus Christ . . . , whom you crucified, whom God raised from the dead . . . BECAME THE CHIEF CORNER stone. And there is salvation in no one else; for there is no other name under heaven that has been given among men by which we must be saved. (Acts 4:10-12)

That fully reliable statement in 1 Timothy tells us that (1) ours was a world full of sinners, (2) the sinners were condemned and needed a Savior, and (3) through His death and resurrection, Jesus (God the Son) came to save

POINT OF INTEREST:[T42]

A WORKER'S GREATEST ASSET—Over the past few decades, employers have demanded increasingly higher levels of academic and professional credentials. During the same time period, however, social scientists have reported *decreasing* levels of job satisfaction. One major reason is that most workers are over-qualified for their jobs. The work employers want done requires far less training than the standards set for their positions. Because advanced degrees and other credentials increase payroll expense, it's been anybody's guess why this trend has continued.

Recently, however, the tide appears to be turning. A president of a local engineering firm offered this explanation: "Fewer and fewer applicants are demonstrating character traits like honesty, responsibility, reliability, loyalty, truthfulness, and so forth. When good character is missing, management simply can't fix it. But a motivated and teachable employee who has foundational skills and good character (including a good work ethic) can be taught to do most any job well. We still aim for good job skills and a good education, of course; but when we have to choose between credentials and character, we're now placing our emphasis on character."

[181]COLOSSIANS 3
12-17 As those who have been chosen of God, holy and beloved, put on a heart of compassion, kindness, humility, gentleness and patience; bearing with one another, and forgiving each other . . . ; just as the Lord forgave you, so also should you. Beyond all these things put on love, which is the perfect bond of unity. Let the peace of Christ rule in your hearts. . . . Whatever you do in word or deed, do all in the name of the Lord Jesus, giving thanks through Him to God the Father.

[182]1 SAMUEL 26
23 The LORD will repay each man for his righteousness and his faithfulness [emunah].

[183]MATTHEW 25
21 "His master said to him, 'Well done, good and faithful slave; you were faithful [pistos] with a few things, I will put you in charge of many things; enter into the joy of your master.' "

[184]LUKE 12
42,44,48 The Lord said, "Who then is the faithful [pistos] and sensible steward. . . . Truly I say to you that he will put him in charge of all his possessions. . . . From everyone who has been given much much will be required; and to whom they entrusted much, of him they will ask all the more."

them. And He is still saving those who have been fully persuaded by the Scriptures so that they've put their full confidence in Christ.

We are saved, then, "not on the basis of deeds which we have done in righteousness, but according to His mercy, by the washing of regeneration and renewing by the Holy Spirit" (Titus 3:5).

Read Romans 6:17-18.[179] What does obedience from the heart and commitment to right teaching also do for us?

Jesus came to set us free from sin, not to make us independent. The same act that releases us from the slavery of sin enslaves us to the Lord in righteousness, peace, and joy in the Holy Spirit (Romans 14:17). When we surrender to Him, He becomes our new Master. How do you feel about being a "slave" to Jesus?

___ Indifferent   ___ Insulted
___ Wanting freedom   ___ Loved
___ Resistant   ___ Other:

Read Philippians 2:5-8.[180] Who was Jesus before He came into the world, and what did He become?

God the Son submitted to being bound in a human body in order to come into the world to set us free from sin. His death atoned for (paid for) our sin debt. To ransom us (buy us back) from the slave market of sin, Jesus willingly became a slave Himself.[T43] Philippians 2:5-8 tells us that His attitude should also be our attitude if we belong to Him.

Read Colossians 3:12-17,[181] paying attention to the attributes of God's chosen and faithful. List the attributes that would contribute to a well-functioning work group.

An employee who is compassionate, kind, humble, gentle, and patient; who would bear with and forgive others; and who would promote unity in the work team would be invaluable. But what does all this have to do with the attribute of faithfulness? Simply this: true and lasting faithfulness can be offered only by bond slaves to Christ. It is His faithfulness in us, in fact, that enables us to be faithful in any of our life roles—child, spouse, parent, neighbor, employee. When work pressures and temptations mount, those who are enslaved to sin will respond as sinners. But those who are enslaved to righteousness can be faithful through the power of His indwelling Spirit.

Servanthood—even slavery—to the Lord is a blessing, not a burden, and it carries two distinctive elements that make it a unique type of slavery.

First, only God's slavery has eternal rewards. Read 1 Samuel 26:23,[182] Matthew 25:21,[183] and Luke 12:42,44,48.[184] What are these rewards?

Second, Jesus has a unique relationship with the faithful slave who is His. Read John 15:14-16.[185] What is this relationship?

The eternal rewards of being God's servant are to share in His joys, to have access to the Lord's possessions, and to have authority in His kingdom. Also, being the Master's slaves means we are His friends. This Greek word for "friend" is *philos,* meaning "dear; beloved." What an honor for the faithful slave to also be the intimate and beloved friend of the King of kings, the Creator God! Though much is required of the faithful slave, much is also given so that the bond slave of God will be fully equipped for the good works for which he or she is appointed.

BRINGING IT HOME

1. Being the slave of Christ means that we do His bidding. List some things you know are the Master's will for your life. How are you doing in your role as a bond slave?

2. Consider the dual nature of your relationship to Christ, that is, your status as His slave and your status as His beloved friend. Do these dual roles make it more or less difficult for you to follow Christ? How could you better reflect your close friendship with Jesus in the workplace?

HISTORY & CULTURE:[T43]

A BOND SLAVE—It is important to distinguish between two ideas of slavery. Being forced into slavery is quite different from submitting to slavery out of love for the slave owner. In Bible times, both types of slavery were common. Certainly there was forced slavery when nations were overthrown by invading governments. But read about a special type of slavery described in Deuteronomy 15:12-13,16-17: "If your kinsman, a Hebrew man or woman, is sold to you, then he shall serve you six years, but in the seventh year you shall set him free. When you set him free, you shall not send him away empty-handed. . . . It shall come about if he says to you, 'I will not go out from you,' because he loves you and your household, since he fares well with you; then you shall take an awl and pierce it through his ear into the door, and he shall be your servant forever."

This bond slave is a picture of our slavery to Christ. Our Master deals kindly with us, even in our sin, and we fare well with Him. Therefore, we willingly become enslaved to the Lord forever, held only by bonds of love.

SCRIPTURE MEDITATION

This I recall to my mind, therefore I have hope. The LORD's loving-kindnesses indeed never cease, for His compassions never fail. They are new every morning; Great is Your faithfulness. 'The LORD is my portion,' says my soul, 'Therefore I have hope in Him.' The LORD is good to those who wait for Him, to the person who seeks Him. (Lamentations 3:21-25)

DAY 2

ATTITUDES OF GOD'S EMPLOYEES

[185]**JOHN 15**

14-16 "You are My friends if you do what I command you. No longer do I call you slaves, for the slave does not know what his master is doing; but I have called you friends, for all things that I have heard from My Father I have made known to you. You did not choose Me but I chose you, and appointed you that you should go and bear fruit, and that your fruit should remain."

[186]**LUKE 2**

40 The Child [Jesus] continued to grow and become strong, increasing in wisdom; and the grace of God was upon Him.

52 And Jesus kept increasing in wisdom and stature, and in favor with God and men.

[187]**HEBREWS 3**

1-2,5-6 Holy brethren, partakers of a heavenly calling, consider Jesus, the Apostle and High Priest of our confession. He was faithful to Him who appointed Him. . . . Now Moses was faithful in all His house as a servant . . . ; but Christ was faithful as a Son over His house—whose house we are, if we hold fast our confidence and the boast of our hope firm until the end.

If our goal is Christlikeness in the workplace, then we need to think about Jesus as a worker. Scripture gives us glimpses of Jesus' personality and character, both in His youth and at the beginning of His public ministry. Read Luke 2:40,52.[186] What was Jesus like in His personal nature?[T44]

Isaiah 53:2 tells us, by way of prophecy, that Jesus would have "no stately form or majesty that we should look upon Him, nor appearance that we should be attracted to Him." Nevertheless, Jesus grew in body (physical strength) and mind (emotional maturity). Jesus also grew intellectually and increased in wisdom, and He so manifested the grace of God that He found favor with both God and people.

Consistent with Jewish culture and tradition, Jesus followed in His earthly "father's" (Joseph's) occupational footsteps (Matthew 13:55). Mark 6:3 tells us explicitly that Jesus worked as a carpenter before He began His public ministry, and He probably worked at this trade for several years.

Imagine the likable, capable Jesus as an employee in His father's shop and perhaps later in a shop of His own. What kind of worker do you think Jesus would have been? (You might want to refer to Hebrews 3:1-2,5-6.[187])

If Jesus was a faithful (thus honest, trustworthy, stable, reliable, and truthful) employee in His heavenly Father's house, then He was a faithful employee in His earthly "father's" shop as well. Consider the following behaviors and think about how Jesus lived out these behaviors.

- He would have treated his superiors with respect.
- He would have arrived at work on time.
- He would have stayed on task.
- He would have put in a fully productive day.
- He would have gotten along with His coworkers and customers.
- He would have produced high-quality work.

Jesus was, no doubt, the most skillful, faithful, and diligent employee the world has ever known. We must assume that, by the time He was fully trained, Jesus was producing one magnificent piece (or one finely constructed building) after another.

If we would serve as worthy ambassadors of Christ in the workplace, then we must aspire to be employees with the same work ethic and commitment to excellence that had to be true of Jesus. And we must exhibit the right attitudes and actions as defined in Scripture.

Several actions and attitudes that should be typical of Christian workers are listed in Ephesians 6:5-8,[188] Colossians 3:22-24,[189] and Titus 2:9-10[190] and 3:1-2.[191] Under the headings below, list those actions and attitudes that are fitting for a Christian employee; then list those that would discredit the kingdom of God and dishonor the King.

Christ-Honoring Attitudes   **Dishonoring Attitudes**

It isn't always easy to be obedient, sincere in heart, well-pleasing, offering goodwill and good faith, considerate, and gentle in the workplace, especially when bosses or coworkers are difficult. But the passages in Colossians 3 and Ephesians 6 tell us that our bosses—even those who are kind—aren't the ones we are really serving. Why not?

Read Galatians 1:10[192] and Luke 16:13.[193] What is wrong with working for the approval of people? That is, why would seeking our bosses' approval be a spiritual error?

CROSS-REFERENCES:[T44]

THE FACE OF JESUS—I keep a number of copies of those sweet, dainty paintings of Jesus (you know, the ones with pale, flawless skin; a keen nose; long, soft, wavy hair; and features so feminine you wonder who was the model). When teaching a class called "Who Is Jesus?" I always begin the first lesson by discussing who Jesus is not. As a visual aid (and to make my point), I hold up one of those copies and then rip it to shreds. The expression on people's faces when I tear up that picture is amazing. It's as if I had just violated something sacred.

Such reactions demonstrate how easily cultural icons get embedded in our theology. All of us, in fact, are quite capable of unconsciously accepting nonsense. But Jesus' physical heritage makes it unlikely that He was fair-skinned and keen-nosed. He lived in a hot, arid country and walked dusty roads. Before He began His ministry, He worked as a carpenter—a job that usually makes men both strong and rugged. Besides, Isaiah 53 expressly tells us that Jesus would not even be handsome, much less "pretty."

It is important that we understand who Jesus is and that we not picture His physical being in ways that are contrary to Scripture. And yet there is an even more important issue concerning the appearance of Jesus—one that is vital to the core of Christian doctrine. Cross-reference Daniel 7:9-10 with Revelation 4:2–5:1, noting who is being described. Cross-reference Daniel 10:5-8 with Revelation 1:10-18 and 5:1-13. Compare your findings with Ezekiel 10:1-14. What do you see? Are you surprised?

[188]**EPHESIANS 6**

5-8 Slaves, be obedient to those who are your masters . . . , in the sincerity of your heart, as to Christ; not by way of eye-service, as men-pleasers, but as slaves of Christ, doing the will of God from the heart. With good will render service, as to the Lord, and not to men, knowing that whatever good thing each one does, this he will receive back from the Lord, whether slave or free.

[189]**COLOSSIANS 3**

22-24 Slaves, in all things obey those who are your masters on earth, not with external service, . . . but with sincerity of heart, fearing the Lord. Whatever you do, do your work heartily, as for the Lord rather than for men; knowing that from the Lord you will receive the reward of the inheritance. It is the Lord Christ whom you serve.

[190]**TITUS 2**

9-10 Urge bondslaves to be subject to their own masters in everything, to be well-pleasing, not argumentative, not pilfering, but showing all good faith that they may adorn the doctrine of God our Savior in every respect.

[191]**TITUS 3**

1-2 Remind them [believers] . . . to be obedient, to be ready for every good deed, to malign no one, to be peaceable, gentle, showing every consideration for all men.

Scripture seems contradictory in its instructions: do obey your masters; don't work for them. How would you explain and unravel this seeming paradox?

Jesus Himself has said that no servant can serve two masters. Therefore, Christians must have but one Master, Jesus Christ. Anything we do for anyone on earth is only at the command of the One who has enslaved us with bonds of love. Nevertheless, in the process of serving our Lord, the needs of those in authority are abundantly met.

In essence, then, the Lord tells us to take instruction from our superiors as if it were from Himself. He tells us to view our work as our service to Him—not as an end product but as an ongoing process—performed for an audience of One. And in the process of our work, we will be "returning our talents increased to the invisible God to use or not use as He sees fit" (Flannery O'Connor, *Voices from the Heart*).

Now go back and read Hebrews 3:5-6.[187] Where was Jesus Christ faithful, and how does that relate to us?

How will we know that God has made His dwelling place in us?

The true product in our work experience is not the work of our hands but the work of God's hands. Work is a place where God wants to shape and mold us into a masterpiece fit for glory, and it's a place where He will use us to win others into His kingdom.

BRINGING IT HOME

1. Listed below are some common temptations in the work-place. Put a check beside each issue that may be an area of temptation for you:[T45]

   ___ Cut corners that devalue the end product
   ___ Call in sick when I'm really not
   ___ Take unfair advantage of a boss or employee
   ___ Bait a customer and then switch output
   ___ Deliberately misrepresent the truth (lie)
   ___ Overcharge clients
   ___ Produce poor-quality work
   ___ Waste time instead of producing at work

2. Evaluate your attitudes and actions with your superiors at work in light of the attitudes and actions listed on page 101. List any changes you think you need to make. Ask God to convict you when you fall into bad habits of wrong actions and attitudes. Ask Him also to increase the good actions and attitudes in your interactions with superiors and coworkers as well.

3. Working as unto the Lord is not easy. We cannot escape the world's value system of recognition, promotion, and compensation. Moreover, we all falter at the idea of leaving the outcome up to God without fretting over what we perceive as failure. Nevertheless, Scripture tells us that the reward is connected to the process alone. Review Ephesians 6:5-8 and Colossians 3:22-24. Write down the reward on a three-by-five-inch card and keep it near your workspace so that you can reorient your thinking when work becomes difficult.

POINT OF INTEREST:[T45]

DRAWING A LINE IN ADVANCE—Trials of our faith will show up at our workplace as various opportunities to play in shades of gray. We will be tempted constantly to go along with the crowd (or with the boss), especially if the stakes for personal advantage are high.

One of the best ways to avoid being trapped by our own desires is to consider our areas of personal weakness. As we examine potential temptations one by one, we should draw a line far enough away from the temptation to provide ourselves with a margin of safety.

Suppose, for example, someone has a weakness in the area of money and is presented with an opportunity to increase profits by padding a contract or cutting corners on quality. That person might determine in advance to confess that temptation to a trusted Christian friend and ask for personal accountability. Or if sexual temptation is an area of weakness, that person might determine never to initiate activities where he or she would be alone with a member of the opposite gender, apart from business.

If we'll draw our lines of conviction in advance, we'll reduce the chances of finding ourselves in compromising situations that could ruin us in the long run.

SCRIPTURE MEDITATION

Finally brethren, whatever is true, whatever is honorable, whatever is right, whatever is pure, whatever is lovely, whatever is of good repute, if there is any excellence and if anything worthy of praise, dwell on these things. (Philippians 4:8)

[192]**GALATIANS 1**

10 Am I now seeking the favor of men, or of God? Or am I striving to please men? If I were still trying to please men, I would not be a bond-servant of Christ.

[193]**LUKE 16**

13 "No servant can serve two masters; for either he will hate the one and love the other, or else he will be devoted to one, and despise the other. You cannot serve God and wealth."

[194]**LUKE 4**

43 [Jesus said,] "I must preach the kingdom of God to the other cities also, for I was sent for this purpose."

[195]**1 JOHN 3**

5,7-8 You know that He appeared in order to take away sins; and in Him there is no sin. . . . Make sure no one deceives you; . . . the one who practices sin is of the devil; for the devil has sinned from the beginning. The Son of God appeared for this purpose, to destroy the works of the devil.

[196]**HEBREWS 2**

17-18 He had to be made like His brethren in all things, so that He might become a merciful and faithful high priest in things pertaining to God, to make propitiation for the sins of the people. For since He Himself was tempted in that which He has suffered, He is able to come to the aid of those who are tempted.

DAY 3

MENTORING GOD'S EMPLOYEES

Building Christian character in the workplace requires the help of a mentor—one who has been a faithful and diligent employee in service to God the Father.

Read Luke 4:43[194] and 1 John 3:5,7-8.[195] (Optional reading in appendix A: Matthew 5:17-18 and 10:32-42, Luke 12:49-53, and John 9:39–10:18.) Write Jesus' job description according to these verses:

Job title:

Responsibility 1:

Responsibility 2:

Responsibility 3:

Summary:

Jesus had a clear agenda. He was to preach the kingdom of God, take away the sins of humankind, and destroy the works of the Devil.

As noted in your optional readings in appendix A from Matthew, Luke, and John, Jesus also came to fulfill the Law, to separate out those who are His, to cast on earth a baptism with fire (the Holy Spirit), to open the eyes of the spiritually blind, to gather "sheep" from every nation, to bring peace in the midst of tribulation, to overcome the world, to impart eternal life, and to completely accomplish the work God gave Him to do. He accomplished it all in a span of about three years![T46]

JESUS' TRAINING FOR MINISTRY

One of the few glimpses we have of Jesus between His birth and His ministry (beginning about age thirty) relates to His early preparation for His calling. Read Luke 4:14-22 from appendix A. In this passage, what was Jesus doing to prepare for His calling? How old was He?

At least as early as age twelve, Jesus had a clear under-standing of His purpose. Jesus was preparing for His ministry by listening to religious teachers and asking them questions. Does it seem unusual to you that God the Son would be learning about Himself and His Father from men? Why or why not?

Reread Philippians 2:5-8.[180] What did Jesus do with His power before coming to earth as a baby?

Read Hebrews 2:17-18[196] and Hebrews 5:8-10.[197] How was God the Son fashioned for His time on earth, and how did He learn what being human was like?

Jesus didn't stop being God during His time on earth, but He "disrobed" Himself of His own divine prerogatives and for a time endured the human experience in every way except sin. That experience included being gifted in His calling, applying Himself to study of the Law and the Prophets (Old Testament Scripture), and relying on the Father to reveal truth and insight.

As we saw in unit 2, Jesus became obedient through suffering so that He might become our High Priest. Read John 16:33–17:26 from appendix A. Briefly summarize some of the blessings Jesus prayed for us in His High Priestly prayer:

POINT OF INTEREST:[T46]

NO SENIORITY IN GOD'S SERVICE—How long you labor in God's vineyard is not the issue; it's what you do with where you are in the time you have. Moses spent eighty years in preparation—forty years in the palaces of Egypt and forty more years in the wilderness. Paul studied at the feet of the teaching rabbi Gamaliel and spent three years in the desert in obscu-rity before becoming the greatest missionary the world has ever known. Even Jesus Himself spent much of His life in preparation for a public ministry that lasted (in the flesh) only about three years.

The economy of God is myste-rious. We may spend most of our lives preparing for a work that may last but a short time span on earth. The good news is that, even when we've spent much of our lives in rebellion to Him, it's never too late to be used of God. And God can restore "the years that the locusts have eaten" (see Joel 2:23-26).

[197]**HEBREWS 5**

8-10 Although He was a Son, He learned obedience from the things which He suffered; and having been made perfect, He became to all those who obey Him the source of eternal salvation; being designated by God as a high priest.

[198]**LUKE 3**

21-22 Now . . . Jesus was also baptized, and while He was praying, . . . the Holy Spirit descended upon Him in bodily form like a dove, and a voice came out of heaven, "You are My beloved Son, in You I am well-pleased."

[199]**MATTHEW 25**

23 "His master said to him, 'Well done, good and faithful slave; you were faithful with a few things, I will put you in charge of many things; enter into the joy of your master.'"

[200]**JOHN 17**

17-18 "Sanctify them in the truth; Your word is truth. As You sent Me into the world, I also have sent them into the world."

[201]**1 PETER 2**

13 Submit yourselves for the Lord's sake to every human institution.

[202]**ROMANS 13**

1-2 There is no authority except from God, and those which exist are established by God. Therefore whoever resists authority has opposed the ordinance of God; and they who have opposed will receive condemnation upon themselves.

Jesus prayed this prayer not just for His disciples but also for those of us who would come to know Him through their word. In this prayer Jesus asked the Father to grant us eternal life, knowledge of Himself, fullness of joy, protection from the enemy, sanctification in the truth, and perfection in unity. Moreover, He prayed for us to be filled with the same love that God had for the Son.

Read Luke 3:21-22.[198] What did God say about His Son, Jesus?

How does this compare with what God will say to us, as illustrated in Jesus' parable regarding the distribution and faithful use of talents (financial resources)? Read the key verse: Matthew 25:23.[199]

If we want God's approval (and we do), then we need to follow Jesus' pattern of faithfulness in our heavenly calling as it plays out in every area of our lives, including our work.

According to John 17:17-18[200] and Hebrews 3:1-2,[187] of what are Christians partakers? Where are they also sent?

Just as Jesus was a partaker of the human experience and was sent into the world by God, so we, too, have been made partakers of Christ's heavenly calling and have been sent into the world by Jesus. And with Him as our Mentor, we cannot fail.

BRINGING IT HOME

1. Do you have a sense that Jesus is available to you as a mentor? List the areas in your work where you feel you need the insight of the One who holds the future in His hands. Get with another Christian coworker or friend and pray over these areas. Ask God for insight on how to pray specifically.

2. Keep a journal of your prayers for mentorship at work, noting both what you've been praying and how the Lord has answered. Refer to it for encouragement when you meet the next obstacle in your workplace.

SCRIPTURE MEDITATION

The end of all things is near; therefore, be of sound judgment and sober spirit for the purpose of prayer. Above all, keep fervent in your love for one another, because love covers a multitude of sins. Be hospitable to one another without complaint. As each one has received a special gift, employ it in serving one another as good stewards of the manifold grace of God. Whoever speaks, is to do so as one who is speaking the utterances of God; whoever serves is to do so as one who is serving by the strength which God supplies; so that in all things God may be glorified through Jesus Christ, to whom belongs the glory and dominion forever and ever. Amen. (1 Peter 4:7-11)

DAY 4

HUMAN RELATIONS AND GOD'S EMPLOYEES

[203] **1 PETER 2**

18-23 Servants, be submissive to your masters with all respect, not only to those who are good and gentle, but also to those who are unreasonable. For this finds favor, if for the sake of conscience toward God a man bears up under sorrows when suffering unjustly. . . . For you have been called for this purpose, since Christ also suffered for you, leaving you an example for you to follow in His steps, . . . and while being reviled, He did not revile in return; while suffering, He uttered no threats, but kept entrusting Himself to Him who judges righteously.

[204] **COLOSSIANS 3**

22-25 Slaves, in all things obey those who are your masters on earth, not with external service, as those who merely please men, but with sincerity of heart, fearing the Lord. Whatever you do, do your work heartily, as for the Lord rather than for men; knowing that from the Lord you will receive the reward of the inheritance. It is the Lord Christ whom you serve. For he who does wrong will receive the consequences of the wrong which he has done, and that without partiality.

[205] **HEBREWS 12**

5-11 "MY SON, DO NOT REGARD LIGHTLY THE DISCIPLINE OF THE LORD, NOR FAINT WHEN YOU ARE REPROVED BY HIM; FOR THOSE WHOM THE LORD LOVES HE DISCIPLINES." . . . It is for discipline that you endure; God deals with you as with sons. . . . He disciplines us for our good, that we may share His holiness. . . . To those who have been trained by it [discipline], afterwards it yields the peaceful fruit of righteousness.

We spent considerable time in unit 4 discussing the responsibilities of the employer, particularly relating to fair wages and fair treatment. In today's study we want to focus on the biblical mandates of being a responsible employee and applying ourselves in our work tasks.

Let's begin with our relationships with our bosses or supervisors. Read 1 Peter 2:13[201] and Romans 13:1-2.[202] The workplace is certainly a "human institution." As employees, how should we respond to our employers?

What happens when we oppose authority?

It is difficult to accomplish complex tasks even when everyone is trying to cooperate. But when one or more persons refuse to take direction, processes break down, confusion and frustration reign, productivity drops, costs rise, and profits sag. Owners are hurt—but so are customers and employees. Working cooperatively is not only biblically sound; it's also sound business for everyone involved.

Scripture tells us how to handle ourselves when we have a difficult and demanding boss. Read 1 Peter 2:18-23[203] and Colossians 3:22-25.[204] How are servants to respond to unreasonable masters?

Recall our Master from day 2 and our Mentor from day 3. How did Jesus respond to difficult people?

Christians are to deal with difficult people like Jesus did—without quarreling, trusting the Father who sees all and judges righteously. This is not easy to do! How does having to suffer unjustly make you feel?

___ Abandoned by God   ___ Frustrated with God
___ Loved by God   ___ Mistreated by God
___ Puzzled at God   ___ Unloved

___ Unappreciated   ___ Misunderstood
___ Mistreated by others   ___ Other:

Trials in our walk with God are not meant to be easy; otherwise, they wouldn't be trials! They are, however, meant to be purposeful. Read excerpts from Hebrews 12:5-11.[205] What do we gain from God's discipline through trials?

Read John 15:1-2.[206] What do you think is meant by "bearing more fruit"? (Hint: see Hebrews 12:5-11.)

Scripture compares the Christian life to a race—one that is not finished until we die.[T47] God disciplines us through trials to train us and to build our endurance so that we might finish the race and finish it well. The more we train, the more we take on His likeness, share in His holiness, grow in righteousness, and produce the fruit of the Spirit. God's discipline, then, is for our good; it's confirmation of His love.

Now, how does it strike you to see yourself as a servant to your employer?

I (Gail) often think I'd rather report directly to God and eliminate the "middleman." The irony is, I do report directly to God. And it is at His command that I serve and submit to the "middleman." My independent, Appalachian nature is humbled and subdued by 1 Samuel 15:23.[207] What is compared to rebellion and insubordination?

If all authority is either bestowed or allowed by God, then rebellion against God-ordained human authority is rebellion against God Himself—a sin of the severity of divination (witchcraft) and idolatry. Does this mean, then, that we are to quietly obey everything we're told to do by anyone in any power position? What do you think?

No one besides God has *ever* been given absolute or limitless authority—not even the prince of this world

POINT OF INTEREST:[T47]

THE VALUE OF POSITION— People are far more than just their work. They are living beings capable of relating to the almighty God. In our places of work, the integration point of our value should be our position as a follower of Christ—an identity gained upward, not downward.

If you see yourself as a product of your heredity and environment, you'll find that you hardly count for anything as the world defines you. Who, after all, will really be remembered one hundred years from now? But Scripture turns the world's system upside-down. It isn't what you *do* that is impressive, but what you've *become* as you experience the process of work. Work is no primrose path. There you will face hardships, disappointments, and disagreements. You will gain and lose promotions and raises. You may even be terminated after a long and successful career.

If your work is your identity, then you'll lose your reason for being. You'll be in crisis when you lose your work position. External values are just too fragile to hang your value on. In God's economy, the ultimate integration point is being a child of the King, and thereby you are measured by eternal values.

[206]JOHN 15

1-2 "I am the true vine, and My Father is the vinedresser. Every branch in Me that does not bear fruit, He takes away; and every branch that bears fruit, He prunes it, so that it may bear more fruit."

[207]1 SAMUEL 15

23 Rebellion is as the sin of divination, and insubordination is as iniquity and idolatry.

[208]2 CHRONICLES 26

16 [When King Uzziah] became strong, his heart was so proud that he acted corruptly, and he was unfaithful to the LORD his God.

18-19,21 [The priests said,] "It is not for you, Uzziah, to burn incense to the LORD, but for the priests, the sons of Aaron who are consecrated to burn incense. . . ." But Uzziah . . . was enraged; and . . . leprosy broke out on his forehead. . . . King Uzziah was a leper to the day of his death.

[209]1 PETER 5:1-3,5

1-3,5 I exhort the elders among you, . . . shepherd the flock of God among you, exercising oversight not under compulsion, but voluntarily . . . ; nor yet as lording it over those allotted to your charge. . . . For GOD IS OPPOSED TO THE PROUD, BUT GIVES GRACE TO THE HUMBLE.

[210]COLOSSIANS 4

1 Masters, grant to your slaves justice and fairness, knowing that you too have a Master in heaven.

(Satan). Therefore, while God extends power and authority to humankind, He also establishes boundaries or limits to that authority. Read 2 Chronicles 26:16,18-19,21.[208] What was King Uzziah's problem, and how did God deal with it?

What were, and what will be, the consequences of pride, heavy-handedness, or extending one's own boundaries of authority, according to 1 Peter 5:1-3,5,[209] Colossians 3:22-25,[204] and Psalms 68 and 75[104] (page 64)?

We're told in Luke 1:51-52 that God has scattered those with proud hearts. He has brought down rulers from their thrones, and those who do wrong will receive the consequences of their wrongdoing.

Beware of high places! Empire building not only diminishes our credibility with people, it also puts us at odds with the Lord. Be it king, priest, CEO, or senior pastor—God has a remedy for those who abuse power. Of what are "masters" or bosses reminded to help them avoid abusing their power, according to Colossians 4:1?[210]

Every power on earth has limits, and everybody on earth has a boss. If a religious leader tries to control our worship, or a governmental leader tries to usurp the law, or a boss demands unethical actions, or a husband insists on immorality—our answer must be a resounding no! We are not required to obey a command that is clearly outside the limits of authority, and we will be backed up in this refusal by the Master.

The balance in obeying God-ordained authority and setting healthy limits may seem difficult to find, and there will be times when it isn't entirely clear where the line should be drawn. Some answers for dealing with those in authority (as well as with coworkers) are found in the following Scripture passages. Read these excerpts prayerfully:

Be of the same mind toward one another; do not be haughty in mind, but associate with the lowly. Do not be wise in your own estimation. . . .

Respect what is right in the sight of all men. If possible, so far as it depends on you, be at peace with all men. . . . Do not be overcome by evil, but overcome evil with good. (Romans 12:16-21)

Act as free men, and do not use your freedom as a covering for evil, but use it as bondslaves of God. Honor all men; love the brotherhood, fear God, honor the king. (1 Peter 2:16-17)

Do nothing from selfishness or empty conceit, but with humility of mind let each of you regard one another as more important than himself; do not merely look out for your own personal interests, but also for the interests of others. (Philippians 2:3-4)

We urge you, brethren, admonish the unruly, encourage the fainthearted, help the weak, be patient with all men. See that no one repays another with evil for evil, but always seek after that which is good for one another and for all men. (1 Thessalonians 5:14-15)

BRINGING IT HOME

1. When we are in trial in a work situation, it is helpful to see that our struggles are not unique. The Psalms are particularly comforting. In Psalm 109, the psalmist David is feeling oppressed and mistreated. He pours out his frustrations to the Lord and then meditates on God's goodness. Read this psalm from appendix A. Can you relate to David's heart? Are you comforted by recalling God's goodness?

2. If there is a particularly difficult coworker or superior in your workplace, write that person's name or initials in a place where you (but no one else) will see it often. Write out a brief prayer of blessing for that person and begin praying this prayer regularly. Also pray that he or she will find significance in God.

SCRIPTURE MEDITATION

Who among you is wise and understanding? Let him show by his good behavior his deeds in the gentleness of wisdom. . . . For where jealousy and selfish ambition exist, there is disorder and every evil thing. But the wisdom from above is first pure, then peaceable, gentle, reasonable, full of mercy and good fruits, unwavering, without hypocrisy. And the seed whose fruit is righteousness is sown in peace by those who make peace. (James 3:13,16-18)

DAY 5

SPIRITUAL RICHES OF GOD'S EMPLOYEES

[211]**ECCLESIASTES 5**
13,15-16 There is a grievous evil which I have seen under the sun: riches being hoarded by their owner to his hurt. . . . He will take nothing from the fruit of his labor that he can carry in his hand. . . . Exactly as a man is born, thus will he die. So what is the advantage to him who toils for the wind?

[212]**LUKE 12**
15,21 [Jesus said,] "Be on your guard against every form of greed; for not even when one has an abundance does his life consist of his possessions. . . . [Foolish] is the man who stores up treasure for himself, and is not rich toward God."

[213]**1 TIMOTHY 6**
9-10 Those who want to get rich fall into temptation and a snare and many foolish and harmful desires which plunge men into ruin and destruction. For the love of money is a root of all sorts of evil, and some by longing for it have wandered away from the faith and pierced themselves with many griefs.

[214]**JONAH 2**
8 Those who regard vain idols forsake their faithfulness.

[215]**REVELATION 3**
17 You say, "I am rich, and have become wealthy, and have need of nothing," and you do not know that you are wretched and miserable and poor and blind and naked.

[216]**ROMANS 11**
33 Oh, the depth of the riches both of the wisdom and knowledge of God! How unsearchable are His judgments and unfathomable His ways!

As we've noted throughout this study, the world's riches do not satisfy long enough or deeply enough. Most of us know this is true, yet we still find ourselves desiring more than we have. Read Luke 18:18-30 from appendix A; then read Ecclesiastes 5:13,15-16[211] and Luke 12:15,21[212] from the Road Map. As you read, note what we are to guard against.

This passage in Luke is not condemning wealth but is pointing out that abundant possessions have a greater tendency to generate greed than they do generosity. How do the rich in these passages finally lose their wealth?

We should certainly work diligently and be good stewards of those things given to us by God, but we can't lose sight of the reality that we won't be taking any of it with us when we die. Seeking for earthly riches is a snare of the enemy. Read Luke 16:13[193] and 1 Timothy 6:9-10.[213]

Seeking to be rich is a deadly game, one that can lead to ruin, destruction, and wandering away from the faith. We can't hoard riches and invest in God's kingdom. We can't think all our desires are satisfied and feel the need for God or look to Him for provision. We simply will not (and cannot) pursue both God and wealth.

ENJOYING WEALTH

Some people are born into money and some marry into money. But there are only two basic ways that people become wealthy through their labors: one is a direct effort to become wealthy as a goal in itself (the worrier); the other is to become wealthy as a byproduct of diligent labors and good stewardship (the worker). The lives of these two types of wealth builders are compared in Ecclesiastes 5:10,12–6:3 (appendix A). In the following chart, compare the worker's accumulation of wealth with the worrier's accumulation of wealth. How are their lives different?[T48]

Worker	Worrier

Wealth can easily come between us and God. When it does, it has become an idol in our lives. Read Jonah 2:8.[214] What do those who regard vain idols forsake?

The NIV Bible translates Jonah 2:8 this way: "Those who cling to worthless idols forfeit the grace that could be theirs." Even if we don't hoard wealth, seeking and putting our trust in it causes us to forsake our Christian character (faithfulness), and it robs us of the peace of God's grace. How foolish it is for us to cling to that which is temporal and that which can never be truly enjoyed without the blessing of the Father!

Read Revelation 3:17[215] What is true about those who think their needs are met in their wealth?

Earthly wealth without God's eternal riches is a delusion. Those who think they're well supplied are trusting in false security. They are spiritually blinded to their own wretchedness, nakedness, and poverty. And they are in desperate need of that which is true riches indeed.

TRUE RICHES

True riches have nothing to do with material or financial possessions. We are told in Romans 10:12 that "the same Lord is Lord of all, abounding in riches for all who call upon Him." What are some of the sources of God's riches according to the following verses?

POINT OF INTEREST:[T48]

POSITIONAL WORTH—When two people meet, they usually (consciously or unconsciously) rank the value of the other on the impressiveness of his or her position. If that seems extreme, consider this: Would you be more likely to defer to the president of Exxon Petroleum or to the guy who pumps the gas in your car? Most people would give greater social weight to the Exxon president. But when they do, they've debased both men, for they've assigned each man's worth on the basis of his position rather than on his value to God.

Our culture encourages us to treat people in ways that have little to do with their true worth. We use all kinds of externals to rate people—race, gender, relative social position, appearance, income, and so forth. Women are often valued for their external beauty and men for their earning potential. But no amount of cosmetics or surgery will hold aging at bay. Likewise, position and income can be lost in a moment. We must make a conscious effort to value ourselves and one another on the basis of our value to our Creator. Anything less is like building one's life on quicksand.

[217]EPHESIANS 1

7,18 In Him we have redemption through His blood, the forgiveness of our trespasses, according to the riches of His grace. . . . I pray that the eyes of your heart may be enlightened, so that you may know what is the hope of His calling, what are the riches of the glory of His inheritance in the saints.

[218]COLOSSIANS 2

2 [I pray they may attain] all the wealth that comes from the full assurance of understanding, resulting in a true knowledge of God's mystery, that is, Christ Himself.

[219]1 TIMOTHY 6

11-12,18 You man of God; . . . pursue righteousness, godliness, faith, love, perseverance and gentleness. Fight the good fight of faith; take hold of the eternal life to which you were called. . . . Be rich in good works, . . . generous and ready to share.

[220]HEBREWS 6

10-12 God is not unjust so as to forget your work and the love which you have shown toward His name, in having ministered and in still ministering to the saints. And we desire that each one of you show the same diligence so as to realize the full assurance of hope until the end, that you will . . . through faith and patience inherit the promises.

<u>Scripture</u>	<u>Source of Riches</u>
Romans 11:33[216]	
Ephesians 1:7,18[217]	
Colossians 2:2[218]	

There are no greater riches than the assurance that comes from understanding Christ, experiencing His grace, having hope in our eternal inheritance, and partaking of the knowledge and wisdom of God. Read a description of divine wisdom from Proverbs 8:12,18-21,34-35:

> I, wisdom, dwell with prudence. . . .
> Riches and honor are with me,
> Enduring wealth and righteousness.
> My fruit is better than gold, even pure gold,
> And my yield better than choicest silver.
> I walk in the way of righteousness,
> In the midst of the paths of justice,
> To endow those who love me with wealth,
> That I may fill their treasuries. . . .
> Blessed is the man who listens to me,
> Watching daily at my gates,
> Waiting at my doorposts.
> For he who finds me finds life,
> And obtains favor from the LORD.

These verses from Proverbs describe true riches. As we are rich in Him, we are also to be rich in our response to Him. Read 1 Timothy 6:11-12,18.[219] Describe the lifestyle of those who are called into the riches of God's kingdom.

Read Hebrews 6:10-12.[220] What has God promised to remember? What has He promised we'll inherit?

How long must we be diligent to realize our hope?

No matter how hard we work, death will still separate us from our earthly treasures. But for those who have diligently labored as unto the Lord, death will be the gateway to the treasures they've laid up in heaven. For the reward of humility and the fear of the Lord are lasting riches, honor, and eternal life (see Proverbs 22:4). Therefore, let not rich people boast of their riches, but let them who boast boast of this: that they understand and know Jesus Christ (see Jeremiah 9:24).[T49]

We have this assurance: God shall supply all our needs according to His riches in glory in Christ Jesus (see Philippians 4:19). As we daily perform our work, then, let us set our sights toward home.

BRINGING IT HOME

1. After your studies in this unit, do you see yourself as God's employee (that is, God's bond slave)? Why or why not?

2. If you do see yourself as God's bond slave, what implications does this have for the quality and purpose of your work?

3. If you do not see yourself as God's bond slave because you have not been born again, read through the verses and instructions provided in appendix B. Pray before you begin, asking God to reveal to you His plan of salvation.

4. We have covered a lot of territory in this study on wisdom at work. Take a few moments to review your workbook. Write down the points that have meant the most to you.

CROSS-REFERENCES:[T49]

TREASURES IN HEAVEN—Most of us get so caught up with our day-to-day responsibilities that we have little time to think about eternity. It is helpful, however, to reflect on our lives in the hereafter. If we are saved, there is much reward waiting for us in heaven.

The following references may give you a better perspective of our eternal reward as well. Be sure to look up any cross-references associated with these passages:

Matthew 6:1-4,19-21; Matthew 7:11; Mark 10:17-30; Luke 6:22-23; John 14:1-21; Hebrews 11:9-10; Philippians 1:21-23; Colossians 1:3-6; Hebrews 11:24-26; 1 Peter 1:3-9; Revelation 21:1–22:7.

SCRIPTURE MEDITATION

"The kingdom of heaven is like a treasure hidden in the field, which a man found and hid again; and from joy over it he goes and sells all that he has and buys that field. Again, the kingdom of heaven is like a merchant seeking fine pearls, and upon finding one pearl of great value, he went and sold all that he had and bought it. . . ." And Jesus said to them, "Therefore every scribe who has become a disciple of the kingdom of heaven is like a head of a household, who brings out of his treasure things new and old." (Matthew 13:44-46,52)

To the leader: For activity 2, you will need a flipchart or board for creating a chart.

1. Faithfulness (as it is described in the Bible) encompasses most of the attributes that employers want in their employees. Because Christians are servants of the Master and have been equipped by Him with the qualities of faithfulness, it follows that we should be attractive as employees.

   • What character qualities do employers generally like to see in their workers? How are these related to faithfulness?

   • Define the biblical terms *emunah* and *pistos* in your own words.

   • What is Christian freedom? What is Christian slavery?

   • Is there a mix of Christians and non-Christians in your workplace? If so, what differences do you see in the way they behave during the workday? (Be honest, and wrestle with the implications of whatever you actually see.)

2. Christians should have the highest work ethic, yet we should view our work not as an end in itself but as a way to serve God. In the end, we are not the ones who are making products, but rather we *are* the products as God shapes us into what He wants us to be.

   • If you were to walk into Joseph & Son's Carpentry Shop in Nazareth to get your plow mended, what do you think you would observe in the shop while you waited?

   • Using a flipchart or board, create a list of wrong and right attitudes and actions, based on the notes you jotted on page 101. Which of the right attitudes and actions seem hardest for Christians to achieve, and why?

   • In practical terms, what does it mean for you to do your work as unto the Lord? Cite examples.

   • How is God molding you through your work?

3. When Jesus was on earth, He had a job to do. He also had training in His childhood so that He could do that job. When He entered upon His ministry, He was successful in accomplishing what He'd come for, and so He received approbation from the Father. In all this, Jesus is a model for us as a worker.

   • What was Jesus' "job"? How was He trained for it? What were the results of His efforts?

   • In what ways can Jesus be a mentor for us as we attempt to serve God in our work?

4. Bosses have God-given authority over their employees (within limits). Therefore, employees should be obedient, at least so long as their bosses' directives are reasonable.

   • Have you ever been in a work situation where one or more employees were refusing to cooperate with the managers? Describe the situation. What was the outcome?

   • Have you ever been in a work situation where obeying your boss became really unpleasant? Describe the situation. As you look back, in what ways was it a growing experience for you?

   • Have you ever been in a work situation where a manager abused his or her authority? Describe the situation.

   • In your opinion, what light do the four scriptural excerpts on page 110-111 shed on the matter of finding a balance between obeying authority and maintaining healthy limits?

5. Material riches don't compare with spiritual riches. If we seek wealth to the neglect of our spiritual well-being, we lose many of the joys that can be ours in this life and riches in the next.

   • An old proverb has it that "Money is a good servant but a bad master." What kinds of things happen to people who allow themselves to be mastered by money?

   • What are the spiritual riches any Christian can have, regardless of how much money he or she possesses?

To close, take turns telling how you plan to change your approach to work as a result of this study. Then intercede for one another in prayer, seeking God's help as group members try to follow through on their intentions. In the days and weeks to come, provide encouragement and accountability for each other.

Appendix A—Scripture Readings

UNIT 1

GENESIS 1–3

1:1 In the beginning God created the heavens and the earth.

1:2 The earth was formless and void, and darkness was over the surface of the deep, and the Spirit of God was moving over the surface of the waters.

1:3 Then God said, "Let there be light"; and there was light.

1:4 God saw that the light was good; and God separated the light from the darkness.

1:5 God called the light day, and the darkness He called night. And there was evening and there was morning, one day.

1:6 Then God said, "Let there be an expanse in the midst of the waters, and let it separate the waters from the waters."

1:7 God made the expanse, and separated the waters which were below the expanse from the waters which were above the expanse; and it was so.

1:8 God called the expanse heaven. And there was evening and there was morning, a second day.

1:9 Then God said, "Let the waters below the heavens be gathered into one place, and let the dry land appear"; and it was so.

1:10 God called the dry land earth, and the gathering of the waters He called seas; and God saw that it was good.

1:11 Then God said, "Let the earth sprout vegetation, plants yielding seed, and fruit trees on the earth bearing fruit after their kind, with seed in them"; and it was so.

1:12 The earth brought forth vegetation, plants yielding seed after their kind, and trees bearing fruit with seed in them, after their kind; and God saw that it was good.

1:13 And there was evening and there was morning, a third day.

1:14 Then God said, "Let there be lights in the expanse of the heavens to separate the day from the night and let them be for signs and for seasons, and for days and years;

1:15 and let them be for lights in the expanse of the heavens to give light on the earth"; and it was so.

1:16 And God made the two great lights, the greater light to govern the day, and the lesser light to govern the night; He made the stars also.

1:17 God placed them in the expanse of the heavens to give light on the earth,

1:18 and to govern the day and the night, and to separate the light from the darkness; and God saw that it was good.

1:19 And there was evening and there was morning, a fourth day.

1:20 Then God said, "Let the waters teem with swarms of living creatures, and let birds fly above the earth in the open expanse of the heavens."

1:21 God created the great sea monsters, and every living creature that moves, with which the waters swarmed after their kind, and every winged bird after its kind; and God saw that it was good.

1:22 God blessed them, saying, "Be fruitful and multiply, and fill the waters in the seas, and let birds multiply on the earth."

1:23 And there was evening and there was morning, a fifth day.

1:24 Then God said, "Let the earth bring forth living creatures after their kind: cattle and creeping things and beasts of the earth after their kind"; and it was so.

1:25 God made the beasts of the earth after their kind, and the cattle after their kind, and everything that creeps on the ground after its kind; and God saw that it was good.

1:26 Then God said, "Let Us make man in Our image, according to Our likeness; and let them rule over the fish of the sea and over the birds of the sky and over the cattle and over all the earth, and over every creeping thing that creeps on the earth."

1:27 God created man in His own image, in the

image of God He created him; male and female He created them.

1:28 God blessed them; and God said to them, "Be fruitful and multiply, and fill the earth, and subdue it; and rule over the fish of the sea and over the birds of the sky and over every living thing that moves on the earth."

1:29 Then God said, "Behold, I have given you every plant yielding seed that is on the surface of all the earth, and every tree which has fruit yielding seed; it shall be food for you;

1:30 and to every beast of the earth and to every bird of the sky and to every thing that moves on the earth which has life, I have given every green plant for food"; and it was so.

1:31 And God saw all that He had made, and behold, it was very good. And there was evening and there was morning, the sixth day.

2:1 Thus the heavens and the earth were completed, and all their hosts.

2:2 By the seventh day God completed His work which He had done, and He rested on the seventh day from all His work which He had done.

2:3 Then God blessed the seventh day and sanctified it, because in it He rested from all His work which God had created and made.

2:4 This is the account of the heavens and the earth when they were created, in the day that the LORD God made earth and heaven.

2:5 Now no shrub of the field was yet in the earth, and no plant of the field had yet sprouted, for the LORD God had not sent rain upon the earth; and there was no man to cultivate the ground.

2:6 But a mist used to rise from the earth and water the whole surface of the ground.

2:7 Then the LORD God formed man of dust from the ground, and breathed into his nostrils the breath of life; and man became a living being.

2:8 The LORD God planted a garden toward the east, in Eden; and there He placed the man whom He had formed.

2:9 Out of the ground the LORD God caused to grow every tree that is pleasing to the sight and good for food; the tree of life also in the midst of the garden, and the tree of the knowledge of good and evil.

2:10 Now a river flowed out of Eden to water the garden; and from there it divided and became four rivers.

2:11 The name of the first is Pishon; it flows around the whole land of Havilah, where there is gold.

2:12 The gold of that land is good; the bdellium and the onyx stone are there.

2:13 The name of the second river is Gihon; it flows around the whole land of Cush.

2:14 The name of the third river is Tigris; it flows east of Assyria. And the fourth river is the Euphrates.

2:15 Then the LORD God took the man and put him into the garden of Eden to cultivate it and keep it.

2:16 The LORD God commanded the man, saying, "From any tree of the garden you may eat freely;

2:17 but from the tree of the knowledge of good and evil you shall not eat, for in the day that you eat from it you shall surely die."

2:18 Then the LORD God said, "It is not good for the man to be alone; I will make him a helper suitable for him."

2:19 Out of the ground the LORD God formed every beast of the field and every bird of the sky, and brought them to the man to see what he would call them; and whatever the man called a living creature, that was its name.

2:20 The man gave names to all the cattle, and to the birds of the sky, and to every beast of the field, but for Adam there was not found a helper suitable for him.

2:21 So the LORD God caused a deep sleep to fall upon the man, and he slept; then He took one of his ribs, and closed up the flesh at that place.

2:22 The LORD God fashioned into a woman the rib which He had taken from the man, and brought her to the man.

2:23 The man said, "This is now bone of my bones, and flesh of my flesh; she shall be called Woman, because she was taken out of Man."

2:24 For this reason a man shall leave his father and his mother, and be joined to his wife; and they shall become one flesh.

2:25 And the man and his wife were both naked and were not ashamed.

3:1 Now the serpent was more crafty than any beast of the field which the LORD God had made. And he said to the woman, "Indeed, has God said, 'You shall not eat from any tree of the garden'?"

3:2 The woman said to the serpent, "From the fruit of the trees of the garden we may eat;

3:3 but from the fruit of the tree which is in the middle of the garden, God has said, 'You shall not eat from it or touch it, or you will die.'"

3:4 The serpent said to the woman, "You surely will not die!

3:5 "For God knows that in the day you eat from it your eyes will be opened, and you will be like God, knowing good and evil."

3:6 When the woman saw that the tree was good for food, and that it was a delight to the eyes, and that the tree was desirable to make one wise, she took from its fruit and ate; and she gave also to her husband with her, and he ate.

3:7 Then the eyes of both of them were opened, and they knew that they were naked; and they sewed fig leaves together and made themselves loin coverings.

3:8 They heard the sound of the LORD God walking in the garden in the cool of the day, and the man and his wife hid themselves from the presence of the LORD God among the trees of the garden.

3:9 Then the LORD God called to the man, and said to him, "Where are you?"

3:10 He said, "I heard the sound of You in the garden, and I was afraid because I was naked; so I hid myself."

3:11 And He said, "Who told you that you were naked? Have you eaten from the tree of which I commanded you not to eat?"

3:12 The man said, "The woman whom You gave to be with me, she gave me from the tree, and I ate."

3:13 Then the LORD God said to the woman, "What is this you have done?" And the woman said, "The serpent deceived me, and I ate."

3:14 The LORD God said to the serpent, "Because you have done this, cursed are you more than all cattle, and more than every beast of the field; on your belly you will go, and dust will you eat all the days of your life;

3:15 And I will put enmity between you and the woman, and between your seed and her seed; He shall bruise you on the head, and you shall bruise him on the heel."

3:16 To the woman He said, "I will greatly multiply your pain in childbirth, in pain you will bring forth children; yet your desire will be for your husband, and he will rule over you."

3:17 Then to Adam He said, "Because you have listened to the voice of your wife, and have eaten from the tree about which I commanded you, saying, 'You shall not eat from it'; cursed is the ground because of you; in toil you will eat of it all the days of your life.

3:18 "Both thorns and thistles it shall grow for you; and you will eat the plants of the field;

3:19 By the sweat of your face you will eat bread, till you return to the ground, because from it you were taken; for you are dust, and to dust you will return."

3:20 Now the man called his wife's name Eve, because she was the mother of all the living.

3:21 The LORD God made garments of skin for Adam and his wife, and clothed them.

3:22 Then the LORD God said, "Behold, the man has become like one of Us, knowing good and evil; and now, he might stretch out his hand, and take also from the tree of life, and eat, and live forever"—

3:23 therefore the LORD God sent him out from the garden of Eden, to cultivate the ground from which he was taken.

3:24 So He drove the man out; and at the east of the garden of Eden He stationed the cherubim, and the flaming sword which turned every direction to guard the way to the tree of life.

REVELATION 21–22

21:1 Then I saw a new heaven and a new earth; for the first heaven and the first earth passed away, and there is no longer any sea.

21:2 And I saw the holy city, new Jerusalem, coming down out of heaven from God, made ready as a bride adorned for her husband.

21:3 And I heard a loud voice from the throne, saying, "Behold, the tabernacle of God is among men, and He will dwell among them, and they shall be His people, and God Himself will be among them.

21:4 and He will wipe away every tear from their eyes; and there will no longer be any death; there will no longer be any mourning, or crying, or pain; the first things have passed away."

21:5 And He who sits on the throne said, "Behold, I am making all things new." And He said, "Write, for these words are faithful and true."

21:6 Then He said to me, "It is done. I am the Alpha and the Omega, the beginning and the end. I will give to the one who thirsts from the spring of the water of life without cost.

21:7 "He who overcomes will inherit these things, and I will be his God and he will be My son.

21:8 "But for the cowardly and unbelieving and abominable and murderers and immoral persons and sorcerers and idolaters and all liars, their part will be in the lake that burns with fire and brimstone, which is the second death."

21:9 Then one of the seven angels who had the seven bowls full of the seven last plagues came and spoke with me, saying, "Come here, I will show you the bride, the wife of the Lamb."

21:10 And he carried me away in the Spirit to a great and high mountain, and showed me the holy city, Jerusalem, coming down out of heaven from God,

21:11 having the glory of God. Her brilliance was like a very costly stone, as a stone of crystal-clear jasper.

21:12 It had a great and high wall, with twelve gates, and at the gates twelve angels; and names were written on them, which are the names of the twelve tribes of the sons of Israel.

21:13 There were three gates on the east and three gates on the north and three gates on the south and three gates on the west.

21:14 And the wall of the city had twelve foundation stones, and on them were the twelve names of the twelve apostles of the Lamb.

21:15 The one who spoke with me had a gold measuring rod to measure the city, and its gates and its wall.

21:16 The city is laid out as a square, and its length is as great as the width; and he measured the city with the rod, fifteen hundred miles; its length and width and height are equal.

21:17 And he measured its wall, seventy-two yards, according to human measurements, which are also angelic measurements.

21:18 The material of the wall was jasper; and the city was pure gold, like clear glass.

21:19 The foundation stones of the city wall were adorned with every kind of precious stone. The first foundation stone was jasper; the second, sapphire; the third, chalcedony; the fourth, emerald;

21:20 the fifth, sardonyx; the sixth, sardious; the seventh, chrysolite; the eighth, beryl; the ninth, topaz; the tenth, chrysoprase; the eleventh, jacinth; the twelfth, amethyst.

21:21 And the twelve gates were twelve pearls; each one of the gates was a single pearl. And the street of the city was pure gold, like transparent glass.

21:22 I saw not temple in it, for the Lord God the Almighty and the lamb are its temple.

21:23 And the city has no need of the sun or of the moon to shine on it, for the glory of God has illumined it, and its lamp is the Lamb.

21:24 The nations will walk by its light, and the kings of the earth will bring their glory into it.

21:25 In the daytime (for there will be no night there) its gates will never be closed;

21:26 and they will bring the glory and the honor of the nations into it;

21:27 and nothing unclean, and no one who practices abomination and lying, shall ever come into it, but only those whose names are written in the Lamb's book of life.

22:1 Then he showed me a river of the water of life, clear as crystal, coming from the throne of God and of the Lamb,

22:2 in the middle of its street. On either side of the river was the tree of life, bearing twelve kinds of fruit, yielding its fruit every month; and the leaves of the tree were for the healing of the nations.

22:3 There will no longer be any curse; and the throne of God and of the Lamb will be in it, and His bond-servants will serve Him;

22:4 they will see His face, and His name will be on their foreheads.

22:5 And there will no longer be any night; and they will not have need of the light of a lamp nor the light of the sun, because the Lord God will illumine them; and they will reign forever and ever.

22:6 And he said to me, "These words are faithful and true"; and the Lord, the God of the spirits of the prophets, send His angel to show to His bond-servants the things which must soon take place.

22:7 "And behold, I am coming quickly. Blessed is he who heeds the words of the prophecy of this book."

22:8 I, John, am the one who heard and saw these things. And when I heard and saw, I fell down to worship at the feet of the angel who showed me these things.

22:9 But he said to me, "Do not do that. I am a fell servant of yours and of your brethren the prophets and of those who heed the words of this book. Worship God."

22:10 And he said to me, "Do not seal up the words of the prophecy of this book, for the time is near.

22:11 "Let the one who does wrong, still do wrong; and the one who is filthy, still be filthy; and let the one who is righteous, still practice righteousness; and the one who is holy, still keep himself holy."

22:12 "Behold, I am coming quickly, and My reward is with Me, to render to every man according to what he has done.

22:13 "I am the Alpha and the Omega, the first and the last, the beginning and the end."

22:14 Blessed are those who wash their robes, so that they may have the right to the tree of life, and may enter by the gates into the city.

22:15 Outside are the dogs and the sorcerers and the immoral persons and the murderers and the idolaters, and everyone who loves and practices lying.

22:16 "I, Jesus, have sent My angel to testify to you these things for the churches. I am the root and the descendant of David, the bright morning star."

22:17 The Spirit and the bride say, "Come." And let the one who hears say, "Come." And let the one who is thirsty come; let the one who wishes take the water of life without cost.

22:18 I testify to everyone who hears the words of the prophecy of this book: if anyone adds to them, God will add to him the plagues which are written in this book;

22:19 and if anyone takes away from the words of the book of this prophecy, God will take away his part from the tree of life and from the holy city, which are written in this book.

22:20 He who testifies to these things says, "Yes, I am coming quickly." Amen. Come, Lord Jesus.

22:21 The grace of the Lord Jesus be with all. Amen.

UNIT 2

MATTHEW 4:17-22

17 From that time Jesus began to preach and say, "Repent, for the kingdom of heaven is at hand."

18 Now as Jesus was walking by the Sea of Galilee, He saw two brothers, Simon who was called Peter, and Andrew his brother, casting a net into the sea; for they were fishermen.

19 And He said to them, "Follow Me, and I will make you fishers of men."

20 Immediately they left their nets and followed Him.

21 Going on from there He saw two other brothers, James the son of Zebedee, and John his brother, in the boat with Zebedee their father, mending their nets; and He called them.

22 Immediately they left the boat and their father and followed Him.

MATTHEW 10:1-4

1 Jesus summoned His twelve disciples and gave them authority over unclean spirits, to cast them out, and to heal every kind of disease and every kind of sickness.

2 Now the names of the twelve apostles are these: The first, Simon, who is called Peter, and Andrew his brother; and James the son of Zebedee, and John his brother;

3 Philip and Bartholomew; Thomas and Matthew the tax collector; James the son of Alphaeus, and Thaddaeus;

4 Simon the Zealot, and Judas Iscariot, the one who betrayed Him.

ACTS 1:6-14

6 So when they had come together, they were asking Him, saying, "Lord, is it at this time You are restoring the kingdom to Israel?"

7 He said to them, "It is not for you to know times or epochs which the Father has fixed by His own authority;

8 but you will receive power when the Holy Spirit has come upon you; and you shall be My witnesses both in Jerusalem, and in all Judea and Samaria, and even to the remotest part of the earth."

9 And after He had said these things, He was lifted up while they were looking on, and a cloud received Him out of their sight.

10 And as they were gazing intently into the sky while He was going, behold, two men in white clothing stood beside them;

11 They also said, "Men of Galilee, why do you stand looking into the sky? This Jesus, who has been taken up from you into heaven, will come in just the same way as you have watched Him go into heaven."

12 Then they returned to Jerusalem from the mount called Olivet, which is near Jerusalem, a Sabbath day's journey away.

13 When they had entered the city, they went up to the upper room where they were staying; that is, Peter and John and James and Andrew, Philip and Thomas, Bartholomew and Matthew, James the son of Alphaeus, and Simon the Zealot, and Judas the son of James.

14 These all with one mind were continually devoting themselves to prayer, along with the women, and Mary the mother of Jesus, and with His brothers.

MATTHEW 16:13-18

13 Now when Jesus came into the district of Caesarea Philippi, He was asking His disciples,

"Who do people say that the Son of Man is?"

14 And they said, "Some say John the Baptist; and others, Elijah; but still others, Jeremiah, or one of the prophets."

15 He said to them, "But who do you say that I am?"

16 Simon Peter answered, "You are the Christ, the Son of the living God."

17 And Jesus said to him, "Blessed are you, Simon Barjona, because flesh and blood did not reveal this to you, but My Father who is in heaven.

18 "I also say to you that you are Peter, and upon this rock I will build My church; and the gates of Hades will not overpower it."

Acts 7:58-59

58 When they had driven him out of the city, they began stoning him; and the witnesses laid aside their robes at the feet of a young man named Saul.

59 They went on stoning Stephen as he called on the Lord and said, "Lord Jesus, receive my spirit!"

Acts 8:1-4

1 Saul was in hearty agreement with putting him to death. And on that day a great persecution arose against the church in Jerusalem, and they were all scattered throughout the regions of Judea and Samaria, except the apostles.

2 Some devout men buried Stephen, and made loud lamentation over him.

3 But Saul began ravaging the church, entering house after house, and dragging off men and women, he would put them in prison.

4 Therefore, those who had been scattered went about preaching the word.

Acts 9:1-22

1 Now Saul, still breathing threats and murder against the disciples of the Lord, went to the high priest,

2 and asked for letters from him to the synagogues at Damascus, so that if he found any belonging to the Way, both men and women, he might bring them bound to Jerusalem.

3 As he was traveling, it happened that he was approaching Damascus, and suddenly a light from heaven flashed around him;

4 and he fell to the ground and heard a voice saying to him, "Saul, Saul, why are you persecuting Me?"

5 And he said, "Who are You, Lord?" And He said, "I am Jesus whom you are persecuting,

6 but get up and enter the city, and it will be told you what you must do."

7 The men who traveled with him stood speechless, hearing the voice but seeing no one.

8 Saul got up from the ground, and though his eyes were open, he could see nothing; and leading him by the hand, they brought him into Damascus.

9 And he was three days without sight, and neither ate nor drank.

10 Now there was a disciple at Damascus named Ananias; and the Lord said to him in a vision, "Ananias." And he said, "Here I am, Lord."

11 And the Lord said to him, "Get up and go to the street called Straight, and inquire at the house of Judas for a man from Tarsus named Saul, for he is praying,

12 and he has seen in a vision a man named Ananias come in and lay his hands on him, so that he might regain his sight."

13 But Ananias answered, "Lord, I have heard from many about this man, how much harm he did to Your saints at Jerusalem;

14 and here he has authority from the chief priests to bind all who call upon Your name."

15 But the Lord said to him, "Go, for he is a chosen instrument of Mine, to bear My name before the Gentiles and kings and the sons of Israel;

16 for I will show him how much he must suffer for My name's sake."

17 So Ananias departed and entered the house, and after laying his hands on him said, "Brother Saul, the Lord Jesus, who appeared to you on the road by which you were coming, has sent me so that you may regain your sight, and be filled with the Holy Spirit."

18 And immediately there fell from his eyes something like scales, and he regained his sight, and he arose and was baptized;

19 and he took food and was strengthened. Now for several days he was with the disciples who were at Damascus,

20 and immediately he began to proclaim Jesus in the synagogues, saying, "He is the Son of God."

21 All those hearing him continued to be amazed, and were saying, "Is this not he who in Jerusalem destroyed those who called on this name, and who had come here for the purpose of bringing them bound before the chief priests?"

22 But Saul kept increasing in strength and confounding the Jews who lived at Damascus by proving that this Jesus is the Christ.

ROMANS 1:1

1 Paul, a bond-servant of Christ Jesus, called as an apostle, set apart for the gospel of God.

GALATIANS 1:1

1 Paul, an apostle (not sent from men nor through the agency of man, but through Jesus Christ and God the Father, who raised Him from the dead).

GENESIS 17:1-12,15-19

1 Now when Abram was ninety-nine years old, the LORD appeared to Abram and said to him, "I am God Almighty; walk before Me, and be blameless.

2 "I will establish My covenant between Me and you, And I will multiply you exceedingly."

3 Abram fell on his face, and God talked with him, saying,

4 "As for Me, behold, My covenant is with you, and you will be the father of a multitude of nations.

5 "No longer shall your name be called Abram, but your name shall be Abraham; for I will make you the father of a multitude of nations.

6 "I will make you exceedingly fruitful, and I will make nations of you, and kings shall come forth from you.

7 "I will establish My covenant between Me and you and your descendants after you throughout their generations for an everlasting covenant, to be God to you and to your descendants after you.

8 "I will give to you and to your descendants after you, the land of your sojournings, all the land of Canaan, for an everlasting possession; and I will be their God."

9 God said further to Abraham, "Now as for you, you shall keep My covenant, you and your descendants after you throughout their generations.

10 "This is My covenant, which you shall keep, between Me and you and your descendants after you: every male among you shall be circumcised.

11 "And you shall be circumcised in the flesh of your foreskin; and it shall be the sign of the covenant between Me and you.

12 "And every male among you who is eight days old shall be circumcised throughout your generations, a servant who is born in the house or who is bought with money from any foreigner, who is not of your descendants.

15 Then God said to Abraham, "As for Sarai your wife, you shall not call her name Sarai, but Sarah shall be her name.

16 "I will bless her, and indeed I will give you a son by her. Then I will bless her, and she shall be a mother of nations; kings of peoples will come from her."

17 Then Abraham fell on his face and laughed, and said in his heart, "Will a child be born to a man one hundred years old? And will Sarah, who is ninety years old, bear a child?"

18 And Abraham said to God, "Oh that Ishmael might live before You!"

19 But God said, "No, but Sarah your wife will bear you a son, and you shall call his name Isaac; and I will establish My covenant with him for an everlasting covenant for his descendants after him."

EXODUS 1:22–2:6,10

1:22 Then Pharaoh commanded all his people, saying, "Every son who is born you are to cast into the Nile, and every daughter you are to keep alive."

2:1 Now a man from the house of Levi went and married a daughter of Levi.

2:2 The woman conceived and bore a son; and when she saw that he was beautiful, she hid him for three months.

2:3 But when she could hide him no longer, she got him a wicker basket and covered it over with tar and pitch. Then she put the child into it and set it among the reeds by the bank of the Nile.

2:4 His sister stood at a distance to find out what would happen to him.

2:5 The daughter of Pharaoh came down to bathe at the Nile, with her maidens walking alongside the Nile; and she saw the basket among the reeds and sent her maid, and she brought it to her.

2:6 When she opened it, she saw the child, and behold, the boy was crying. And she had pity on him and said, "This is one of the Hebrews' children."

2:10 The child grew, and she brought him to Pharaoh's daughter and he became her son. And she named him Moses, and said, "Because I drew him out of the water."

EXODUS 2:23-25

23 Now it came about in the course of those many days that the king of Egypt died. And the sons of Israel sighed because of the bondage, and they cried out; and their cry for help because of their bondage rose up to God.

24 So God heard their groaning; and God remembered His covenant with Abraham, Isaac, and Jacob.

25 God saw the sons of Israel, and God took notice of them.

EXODUS 3:1-12

1 Now Moses was pasturing the flock of Jethro his father-in-law, the priest of Midian; and he led the flock to the west side of the wilderness, and came to Horeb, the mountain of God.

2 The angel of the LORD appeared to him in a blazing fire from the midst of a bush; and he looked, and behold, the bush was burning with fire, yet the bush was not consumed.

3 So Moses said, "I must turn aside now and see this marvelous sight, why the bush is not burned up."

4 When the LORD saw that he turned aside to look, God called to him from the midst of the bush, and said, "Moses, Moses!" And he said, "Here I am."

5 Then He said, "Do not come near here; remove your sandals from your feet, for the place on which you are standing is holy ground."

6 He said also, "I am the God of your father, the God of Abraham, the God of Isaac, and the God of Jacob." Then Moses hid his face, for he was afraid to look at God.

7 The LORD said, "I have surely seen the affliction of My people who are in Egypt, and have given heed to their cry because of their taskmasters, for I am aware of their sufferings.

8 "So I have come down to deliver them from the power of the Egyptians, and to bring them up from that land to a good and spacious land, to a land flowing with milk and honey, to the place of the Canaanite and the Hittite and the Amorite and the Perizzite and the Hivite and the Jebusite.

9 "Now, behold, the cry of the sons of Israel has come to Me; furthermore, I have seen the oppression with which the Egyptians are oppressing them.

10 "Therefore, come now, and I will send you to Pharaoh, so that you may bring My people, the sons of Israel, out of Egypt."

11 But Moses said to God, "Who am I, that I should go to Pharaoh, and that I should bring the sons of Israel out of Egypt?"

12 And He said, "Certainly I will be with you, and this shall be the sign to you that it is I who have sent you: when you have brought the people out of Egypt, you shall worship God at this mountain."

EXODUS 7:2,6-7

1 Then the LORD said to Moses, "See, I make you as God to Pharaoh, and your brother Aaron shall be your prophet.

2 "You shall speak all that I command you, and your brother Aaron shall speak to Pharaoh that he let the sons of Israel go out of his land."

6 So Moses and Aaron did it; as the LORD commanded them, thus they did.

7 Moses was eighty years old and Aaron eighty-three, when they spoke to Pharaoh.

UNIT 3

1 CORINTHIANS 1:18–2:16

1:18 For the word of the cross is foolishness to those who are perishing, but to us who are being saved it is the power of God.

1:19 For it is written, "I WILL DESTROY THE WISDOM OF THE WISE, AND THE CLEVERNESS OF THE CLEVER I WILL SET ASIDE."

1:20 Where is the wise man? Where is the scribe? Where is the debater of this age? Has not God made foolish the wisdom of the world?

1:21 For since in the wisdom of God the world through its wisdom did not come to know God, God was well-pleased through the foolishness of the message preached to save those who believe.

1:22 For indeed Jews ask for signs and Greeks search for wisdom;

1:23 but we preach Christ crucified, to Jews a stumbling block, and to Gentiles foolishness,

1:24 but to those who are the called, both Jews and Greeks, Christ the power of God and the wisdom of God.

1:25 Because the foolishness of God is wiser than men, and the weakness of God is stronger than men.

1:26 For consider your calling, brethren, that there were not many wise according to the flesh, not many mighty, not many noble;

1:27 but God has chosen the foolish things of the world to shame the wise, and God has chosen the weak things of the world to shame the things which are strong,

1:28 and the base things of the world and the despised God has chosen, the things that are not, so that He might nullify the things that are,

1:29 so that no man may boast before God.

1:30 But by His doing you are in Christ Jesus, who became to us wisdom from God, and righteousness and sanctification, and redemption,

1:31 so that, just as it is written, "LET HIM WHO BOASTS, BOAST IN THE LORD."

2:1 And when I came to you, brethren, I did not come with superiority of speech or of wisdom, proclaiming to you the testimony of God.

2:2 For I determined to know nothing among you except Jesus Christ, and Him crucified.

2:3 I was with you in weakness and in fear and in much trembling.

2:4 and my message and my preaching were not in persuasive words of wisdom, but in demonstration of the Spirit and of power,

2:5 so that your faith would not rest on the wisdom of men, but on the power of God.

2:6 Yet we do speak wisdom among those who are mature; a wisdom, however, not of this age nor of the rulers of this age, who are passing away;

2:7 but we speak God's wisdom in a mystery, the hidden wisdom, which God predestined before the ages to our glory;

2:8 the wisdom which none of the rulers of this age has understood; for if they had understood it they would not have crucified the Lord of glory;

2:9 but just as it is written, "THINGS WHICH EYE HAS NOT SEEN AND EAR HAS NOT HEARD, AND WHICH HAVE NOT ENTERED THE HEART OF MAN, ALL THAT GOD HAS PREPARED FOR THOSE WHO LOVE HIM."

2:10 For to us God revealed them through the Spirit; for the Spirit searches all things, even the depths of God.

2:11 For who among men knows the thoughts of a man except the spirit of the man which is in him? Even so the thoughts of God no one knows except the Spirit of God.

2:12 Now we have received, not the spirit of the world, but the Spirit who is from God, so that we may know the things freely given to us by God,

2:13 which things we also speak, not in words taught by human wisdom, but in those taught by the Spirit, combining spiritual thoughts with spiritual words.

2:14 But a natural man does not accept the things of the Spirit of God; for they are foolishness to him, and he cannot understand them, because they are spiritually appraised.

2:15 But he who is spiritual appraises all things, yet he himself is appraised by no man.

2:16 FOR WHO HAS KNOWN THE MIND OF THE LORD, THAT HE SHOULD INSTRUCT HIM? But we have the mind of Christ.

2 SAMUEL 7:8-29

8 "Now therefore, thus you shall say to My servant David, 'Thus says the LORD of hosts, "I took you from the pasture, from following the sheep, to be ruler over My people Israel.

9 "I have been with you wherever you have gone and have cut off all your enemies from before you; and I will make you a great name, like the names of the great men who are on the earth.

10 "I will also appoint a place for My people Israel and will plant them, that they may live in their own place and not be disturbed again, nor will the wicked afflict them any more as formerly,

11 even from the day that I commanded judges to be over My people Israel; and I will give you rest from all your enemies. The LORD also declares to you that the LORD will make a house for you.

12 "When your days are complete and you lie down with your fathers, I will raise up your descendant after you, who will come forth from you, and I will establish his kingdom.

13 "He shall build a house for My name, and I will establish the throne of his kingdom forever.

14 "I will be a father to him and he will be a son to Me; when he commits iniquity, I will correct him with the rod of men and the strokes of the sons of men,

15 but My lovingkindness shall not depart from him, as I took it away from Saul, whom I removed from before you.

16 "Your house and your kingdom shall endure before Me forever; your throne shall be established forever." ' "

17 In accordance with all these words and all this vision, so Nathan spoke to David.

18 Then David the king went in and sat before the LORD, and he said, "Who am I, O Lord GOD, and what is my house, that You have brought me this far?

19 "And yet this was insignificant in Your eyes, O Lord GOD, for You have spoken also of the house of Your servant concerning the distant future. And this is the custom of man, O Lord GOD.

20 "Again what more can David say to You? For

You know Your servant, O Lord GOD!

21 "For the sake of Your word, and according to Your own heart, You have done all this greatness to let Your servant know.

22 "For this reason You are great, O Lord GOD; for there is none like You, and there is no God besides You, according to all that we have heard with our ears.

23 "And what one nation on the earth is like Your people Israel, whom God went to redeem for Himself as a people and to make a name for Himself, and to do a great thing for You and awesome things for Your land, before Your people whom You have redeemed for Yourself from Egypt, from nations and their gods?

24 "For You have established for Yourself Your people Israel as Your own people forever, and You, O LORD, have become their God.

25 "Now therefore, O LORD God, the word that You have spoken concerning Your servant and his house, confirm it forever, and do as You have spoken,

26 that Your name may be magnified forever, by saying, 'The LORD of hosts is God over Israel'; and may the house of Your servant David be established before You.

27 "For You, O LORD of hosts, the God of Israel, have made a revelation to Your servant, saying, 'I will build you a house'; therefore Your servant has found courage to pray this prayer to You.

28 "Now, O Lord GOD, You are God, and Your words are truth, and You have promised this good thing to Your servant.

29 "Now therefore may it please You to bless the house of Your servant, that it may continue forever before You. For You, O Lord GOD, have spoken; and with Your blessing may the house of Your servant be blessed forever."

JEREMIAH 25:9,11-12

8 "Therefore thus says the LORD of hosts, 'Because you have not obeyed My words,

9 behold, I will send and take all the families of the north,' declares the LORD, 'and I will send to Nebuchadnezzar king of Babylon, My servant, and will bring them against this land and against its inhabitants and against all these nations round about; and I will utterly destroy them and make them a horror and a hissing, and an everlasting desolation.

11 'This whole land will be a desolation and a horror, and these nations will serve the king of Babylon seventy years.

12 'Then it will be when seventy years are completed I will punish the king of Babylon and that nation,' declares the LORD, 'for their iniquity, and the land of the Chaldeans; and I will make it an everlasting desolation.'"

DANIEL 4:28–5:6,13-31

4:28 "All this happened to Nebuchadnezzar the king.

4:29 "Twelve months later he was walking on the roof of the royal palace of Babylon.

4:30 "The king reflected and said, 'Is this not Babylon the great, which I myself have built as a royal residence by the might of my power and for the glory of my majesty?'

4:31 "While the word was in the king's mouth, a voice came from heaven, saying, 'King Nebuchadnezzar, to you it is declared: sovereignty has been removed from you,

4:32 and you will be driven away from mankind, and your dwelling place will be with the beasts of the field. You will be given grass to eat like cattle, and seven periods of time will pass over you, until you recognize that the Most High is ruler over the realm of mankind, and bestows it on whomever He wishes.'

4:33 "Immediately the word concerning Nebuchadnezzar was fulfilled; and he was driven away from mankind and began eating grass like cattle, and his body was drenched with the dew of heaven until his hair had grown like eagles' feathers and his nails like birds' claws.

4:34 "But at the end of that period I, Nebuchadnezzar, raised my eyes toward heaven, and my reason returned to me, and I blessed the Most High and praised and honored Him who lives forever; for His dominion is an everlasting dominion, and His kingdom endures from generation to generation.

4:35 "All the inhabitants of the earth are accounted as nothing, but He does according to His will in the host of heaven and among the inhabitants of earth; and no one can ward off His hand or say to Him, 'What have You done?'

4:36 "At that time my reason returned to me. And my majesty and splendor were restored to me for the glory of my kingdom, and my counselors and my nobles began seeking me out; so I was reestablished in my sovereignty, and surpassing greatness was added to me.

4:37 "Now I, Nebuchadnezzar, praise, exalt and honor the King of heaven, for all His works are true and His ways just, and He is able to humble those who walk in pride."

5:1 Belshazzar the king held a great feast for a thousand of his nobles, and he was drinking wine in the presence of the thousand.

5:2 When Belshazzar tasted the wine, he gave orders to bring the gold and silver vessels which Nebuchadnezzar his father had taken out of the temple which was in Jerusalem, so that the king and his nobles, his wives and his concubines might drink from them.

5:3 Then they brought the gold vessels that had been taken out of the temple, the house of God which was in Jerusalem; and the king and his nobles, his wives and his concubines drank from them.

5:4 They drank the wine and praised the gods of gold and silver, of bronze, iron, wood and stone.

5:5 Suddenly the fingers of a man's hand emerged and began writing opposite the lamp-stand on the plaster of the wall of the king's palace, and the king saw the back of the hand that did the writing.

5:6 Then the king's face grew pale and his thoughts alarmed him, and his hip joints went slack and his knees began knocking together.

5:13 Then Daniel was brought in before the king. The king spoke and said to Daniel, "Are you that Daniel who is one of the exiles from Judah, whom my father the king brought from Judah?

5:14 "Now I have heard about you that a spirit of the gods is in you, and that illumination, insight and extraordinary wisdom have been found in you.

5:15 "Just now the wise men and the conjurers were brought in before me that they might read this inscription and make its interpretation known to me, but they could not declare the interpretation of the message.

5:16 "But I personally have heard about you, that you are able to give interpretations and solve difficult problems. Now if you are able to read the inscription and make its interpretation known to me, you will be clothed with purple and wear a necklace of gold around your neck, and you will have authority as the third ruler in the kingdom."

5:17 Then Daniel answered and said before the king, "Keep your gifts for yourself or give your rewards to someone else; however, I will read the inscription to the king and make the interpretation known to him.

5:18 "O king, the Most High God granted sovereignty, grandeur, glory and majesty to Nebuchadnezzar your father.

5:19 "Because of the grandeur which He bestowed on him, all the peoples, nations and men of every language feared and trembled before him; whomever he wished he killed and whomever he wished he spared alive; and whomever he wished he elevated and whomever he wished he humbled.

5:20 "But when his heart was lifted up and his spirit became so proud that he behaved arrogantly, he was deposed from his royal throne, and his glory was taken away from him.

5:21 "He was also driven away from mankind, and his heart was made like that of beasts, and his dwelling place was with the wild donkeys. He was given grass to eat like cattle, and his body was drenched with the dew of heaven until he recognized that the Most High God is ruler over the realm of mankind and that He sets over it whomever He wishes.

5:22 "Yet you, his son, Belshazzar, have not humbled your heart, even though you knew all this,

5:23 but you have exalted yourself against the Lord of heaven; and they have brought the vessels of His house before you, and you and your nobles, your wives and your concubines have been drinking wine from them; and you have praised the gods of silver and gold, of bronze, iron, wood and stone, which do not see, hear or understand. But the God in whose hand are your life-breath and your ways, you have not glorified.

5:24 "Then the hand was sent from Him, and this inscription was written out.

5:25 "Now this is the inscription that was written out: 'MENĒ, MENĒ, TEKĒL, UPHARSIN.'

5:26 "This is the interpretation of the message: 'MENĒ'—God has numbered your kingdom and put an end to it.

5:27 " 'TEKĒL'—you have been weighed on the scales and found deficient.

5:28 " 'PERĒS'—your kingdom has been divided and given over to the Medes and Persians."

5:29 Then Belshazzar gave orders, and they clothed Daniel with purple and put a necklace of gold around his neck, and issued a proclamation concerning him that he now had authority as the third ruler in the kingdom.

5:30 That same night Belshazzar the Chaldean king was slain.

5:31 So Darius the Mede received the kingdom at about the age of sixty-two.

HABAKKUK 1:2-7,11,13

2 How long, O LORD, will I call for help, and You will not hear? I cry out to You, "Violence!" Yet You do not save.

3 Why do You make me see iniquity, . . . Yes, destruction and violence are before me; strife exists . . .

4 Therefore, the law is ignored . . . the wicked surround the righteous; therefore, justice comes out perverted.

5 "Look among the nations! Observe! . . . Because I am doing something in your days—You would not believe. . . .

6 "For behold, I am raising up the Chaldeans, that fierce and impetuous people. . . .

7 Their justice and authority originate with themselves. . . .

11 They will sweep through like the wind and pass on. But they will be held guilty, they whose strength is their god."

13 Your eyes are too pure to approve evil, and You can not look on wickedness with favor. Why do You look with favor on those who deal treacherously? Why are You silent when the wicked swallow up those more righteous than they?

UNIT 4

JOB 20:4-23,26-29

4 "Do you know this from of old, from the establishment of man on earth,

5 That the triumphing of the wicked is short, and the joy of the godless momentary?

6 "Though his loftiness reaches the heavens, and his head touches the clouds,

7 He perishes forever like his refuse; those who have seen him will say, 'Where is he?'

8 "He flies away like a dream, and they cannot find him; even like a vision of the night he is chased away.

9 "The eye which saw him sees him no more, and his place no longer beholds him.

10 "His sons favor the poor, and his hands give back his wealth.

11 "His bones are full of his youthful vigor, but it lies down with him in the dust.

12 "Though evil is sweet in his mouth, and he hides it under his tongue,

13 Though he desires it and will not let it go, but holds it in his mouth,

14 Yet his food in his stomach is changed to the venom of cobras within him.

15 "He swallows riches, but will vomit them up; God will expel them from his belly.

16 "He sucks the poison of cobras; the viper's tongue slays him.

17 "He does not look at the streams, the rivers flowing with honey and curds.

18 "He returns what he has attained and cannot swallow it; as to the riches of his trading, he cannot even enjoy them.

19 "For he has oppressed and forsaken the poor; he has seized a house which he has not built.

20 "Because he knew no quiet within him he does not retain anything he desires.

21 "Nothing remains for him to devour, therefore his prosperity does not endure.

22 "In the fulness of his plenty he will be cramped; the hand of everyone who suffers will come against him.

23 "When he fills his belly, God will send His fierce anger on him and will rain it on him while he is eating.

26 Complete darkness is held in reserve for his treasures, and unfanned fire will devour him; It will consume the survivor in his tent.

27 "The heavens will reveal his iniquity, and the earth will rise up against him.

28 "The increase of his house will depart; his possessions will flow away in the day of His anger.

29 "This is the wicked man's portion from God, even the heritage decreed to him by God."

PSALM 15:1-5

1 O LORD, who may abide in Your tent? Who may dwell on Your holy hill?

2 He who walks with integrity, and works righteousness, and speaks truth in his heart.

3 He does not slander with his tongue, nor does evil to his neighbor, nor takes up a reproach against his friend;

4 in whose eyes a reprobate is despised, but who honors those who fear the LORD; he swears to his own hurt, and does not change;

5 he does not put out his money at interest, nor does he take a bribe against the innocent. He who does these things will never be shaken.

DEUTERONOMY 28:1-25,38-45

1 "Now it shall be, if you diligently obey the LORD your God, being careful to do all His commandments which I command you today, the LORD your God will set you high above all the nations of the earth.

2 "All these blessings will come upon you and overtake you if you obey the LORD your God.

3 "Blessed shall you be in the city, and blessed shall you be in the country.

4 "Blessed shall be the offspring of your body and the produce of your ground and the offspring of your beasts, the increase of your herd and the young of your flock.

5 "Blessed shall be your basket and your kneading bowl.

6 "Blessed shall you be when you come in, and blessed shall you be when you go out.

7 "The LORD shall cause your enemies who rise up against you to be defeated before you; they will come out against you one way and will flee before you seven ways.

8 "The LORD will command the blessing upon you in your barns and in all that you put your hand to, and He will bless you in the land which the LORD your God gives you.

9 "The LORD will establish you as a holy people to Himself, as He swore to you, if you will keep the commandments of the LORD your God and walk in His ways.

10 "So all the peoples of the earth will see that you are called by the name of the LORD, and they will be afraid of you.

11 "The LORD will make you abound in prosperity, in the offspring of your body and in the offspring of your beast and in the produce of your ground, in the land which the LORD swore to your fathers to give you.

12 "The LORD will open for you His good storehouse, the heavens, to give rain to your land in its season and to bless all the work of your hand; and you shall lend to many nations, but you shall not borrow.

13 "The LORD will make you the head and not the tail, and you only will be above, and you will not be underneath, if you listen to the commandments of the LORD your God, which I charge you today, to observe them carefully,

14 and do not turn aside from any of the words which I command you today, to the right or to the left, to go after other gods to serve them.

15 "But it shall come about, if you will not obey the LORD your God, to observe to do all His commandments and His statutes with which I charge you today, that all these curses will come upon you and overtake you:

16 "Cursed shall you be in the city, and cursed shall you be in the country.

17 "Cursed shall be your basket and your kneading bowl.

18 "Cursed shall be the offspring of your body and the produce of your ground, the increase of your herd and the young of your flock.

19 "Cursed shall you be when you come in, and cursed shall you be when you go out.

20 "The LORD will send upon you curses, confusion, and rebuke, in all you undertake to do, until you are destroyed and until you perish quickly, on account of the evil of your deeds, because you have forsaken Me.

21 "The LORD will make the pestilence cling to you until He has consumed you from the land where you are entering to possess it.

22 "The LORD will smite you with consumption and with fever and with inflammation and with fiery heat and with the sword and with blight and with mildew, and they shall pursue you until you perish.

23 "The heaven which is over your head shall be bronze, and the earth which is under you, iron.

24 "The LORD will make the rain of your land powder and dust; from heaven it shall come down on you until you are destroyed.

25 "The LORD shall cause you to be defeated before your enemies; you will go out one way against them, but you will flee seven ways before them, and you will be an example of terror to all the kingdoms of the earth. . . .

38 "You shall bring out much seed to the field but you shall gather in little, for the locust will consume it.

39 "You shall plant and cultivate vineyards, but you will neither drink of the wine nor gather the grapes, for the worm will devour them.

40 "You shall have olive trees throughout your territory but you will not anoint yourself with the oil, for your olives will drop off.

41 "You shall have sons and daughters but they will not be yours, for they will go into captivity.

42 "The cricket shall possess all your trees and the produce of your ground.

43 "The alien who is among you shall rise above you higher and higher, but you will go down lower and lower.

44 "He shall lend to you, but you will not lend to him; he shall be the head, and you will be the tail.

45 "So all these curses shall come on you and pursue you and overtake you until you are destroyed, because you would not obey the LORD your God by keeping His commandments and His statutes which He commanded you."

Psalm 73

1 Surely God is good to Israel, to those who are pure in heart!

2 But as for me, my feet came close to stumbling; my steps had almost slipped.

3 For I was envious of the arrogant, as I saw the prosperity of the wicked.

4 For there are no pains in their death; and their body is fat.

5 They are not in trouble as other men; nor are they plagued like mankind.

6 Therefore pride is their necklace; the garment of violence covers them.

7 Their eye bulges from fatness; the imaginations of their heart run riot.

8 They mock, and wickedly speak of oppression; they speak from on high.

9 They have set their mouth against the heavens, and their tongue parades through the earth.

10 Therefore his people return to this place; and waters of abundance are drunk by them.

11 They say, "How does God know? And is there knowledge with the Most High?"

12 Behold, these are the wicked; and always at ease, they have increased in wealth.

13 Surely in vain I have kept my heart pure, and washed my hands in innocence;

14 For I have been stricken all day long, and chastened every morning.

15 If I had said, "I will speak thus"; behold, I should have betrayed the generation of Your children.

16 When I pondered to understand this, it was troublesome in my sight

17 Until I came into the sanctuary of God; then I perceived their end.

18 Surely You set them in slippery places; You cast them down to destruction.

19 How they are destroyed in a moment! They are utterly swept away by sudden terrors!

20 Like a dream when one awakes, O Lord, when aroused, You will despise their form.

21 When my heart was embittered, and I was pierced within,

22 Then I was senseless and ignorant; I was like a beast before You.

23 Nevertheless I am continually with You; You have taken hold of my right hand.

24 With Your counsel You will guide me, and afterward receive me to glory.

25 Whom have I in heaven but You? And besides You, I desire nothing on earth.

26 My flesh and my heart may fail, but God is the strength of my heart and my portion forever.

27 For, behold, those who are far from You will perish; You have destroyed all those who are unfaithful to You.

28 But as for me, the nearness of God is my good; I have made the Lord GOD my refuge, That I may tell of all Your works.

Luke 5:1-7,11

1 Now it happened that while the crowd were pressing around Him and listening to the word of God, He was standing by the lake of Gennesaret;

2 and He saw two boats lying at the edge of the lake; but the fishermen had gotten out of them, and were washing their nets.

3 And He got into one of the boats, which was Simon's, and asked him to put out a little way from the land. And He sat down and began teaching the people from the boat.

4 When He had finished speaking, He said to Simon, "Put out into the deep water and let down your nets for a catch."

5 Simon answered and said, "Master, we worked hard all night and caught nothing, but I will do as You say and let down the nets."

6 When they had done this, they enclosed a great quantity of fish, and their nets began to break;

7 so they signaled to their partners in the other boat for them to come and help them. And they came and filled both of the boats, so that they began to sink.

11 When they had brought their boats to land, they left everything and followed Him.

Matthew 20:1-16

1 "For the kingdom of heaven is like a landowner who went out early in the morning to hire laborers for his vineyard.

2 "When he had agreed with the laborers for a denarius for the day, he sent them into his vineyard.

3 "And he went out about the third hour and saw others standing idle in the market place;

4 and to those he said, 'You too go into the vineyard, and whatever is right I will give you.' And so they went.

5 "Again he went out about the sixth and the ninth hour, and did the same thing.

6 "And about the eleventh hour he went out, and found others standing around; and he said to them, 'Why have you been standing here idle all day long?'

7 "They said to him, 'Because no one hired us.'
He said to them, 'You go into the vineyard too.'

8 "When evening came, the owner of the vineyard said to his foreman, 'Call the laborers and pay them their wages, beginning with the last group to the first.'

9 "When those hired about the eleventh hour came, each one received a denarius.

10 "When those hired first came, they thought that they would receive more; but each of them also received a denarius.

11 "When they received it, they grumbled at the landowner,

12 saying, 'These last men have worked only one hour, and you have made them equal to us who have borne the burden and the scorching heat of the day.'

13 "But he answered and said to one of them, 'Friend, I am doing you no wrong; did you not agree with me for a denarius?

14 'Take what is yours and go your way, but I wish to give to this last man the same as to you.

15 'Is it not lawful for me to do what I wish with what is my own? Or is your eye envious because I am generous?'

16 "So the last shall be first, and the first last."

UNIT 5

LUKE 12:15-21

15 Then He said to them, "Beware, and be on your guard against every form of greed; for not even when one has an abundance does his life consist of his possessions."

16 And He told them a parable, saying, "The land of a certain rich man was very productive.

17 "And he began reasoning to himself, saying, 'What shall I do, since I have no place to store my crops?'

18 "Then he said, 'This is what I will do: I will tear down my barns and build larger ones, and there I will store all my grain and my goods.

19 'And I will say to my soul, "Soul, you have many goods laid up for many years to come; take your ease, eat, drink and be merry."'

20 "But God said to him, 'You fool! This very night your soul is required of you; and now who will own what you have prepared?'

21 "So is the man who lays up treasure for himself, and is not rich toward God."

MATTHEW 5:17-18; 10:32-42

5:17 "Do not think that I came to abolish the Law or the Prophets; I did not come to abolish but to fulfill.

5:18 "For truly I say to you, until heaven and earth pass away, not the smallest letter or stroke shall pass away from the Law, until all is accomplished.

10:32 "Therefore everyone who confesses Me before men, I will also confess him before My Father who is in heaven.

10:33 "But whoever denies Me before men, I will also deny him before My Father who is in heaven.

10:34 "Do not think that I came to bring peace on the earth; I did not come to bring peace, but a sword.

10:35 "For I came to SET A MAN AGAINST HIS FATHER, AND A DAUGHTER AGAINST HER MOTHER, AND A DAUGHTER-IN-LAW AGAINST HER MOTHER-IN-LAW;

10:36 and A MAN'S ENEMIES WILL BE THE MEMBERS OF HIS HOUSEHOLD.

10:37 "He who loves father or mother more than Me is not worthy of Me; and he who loves son or daughter more than Me is not worthy of Me.

10:38 "And he who does not take his cross and follow after Me is not worthy of Me.

10:39 "He who has found his life shall lose it, and he who has lost his life for My sake will find it.

10:40 "He who receives you receives Me, and he who receives Me receives Him who sent Me.

10:41 "He who receives a prophet in the name of a prophet shall receive a prophet's reward; and he who receives a righteous man in the name of a righteous man shall receive a righteous man's reward.

10:42 "And whoever in the name of a disciple gives to one of these little ones even a cup of cold water to drink, truly I say to you, he shall not lose his reward."

LUKE 12:49-53

49 "I have come to cast fire upon the earth; and how I wish it were already kindled!

50 "But I have a baptism to undergo, and how distressed I am until it is accomplished!

51 "Do you suppose that I came to grant peace on earth? I tell you, no, but rather division;

52 for from now on five members in one household will be divided, three against two, and two against three.

53 "They will be divided, father against son and son against father; mother against daughter and daughter against mother; mother-in-law against daughter-in-law and daughter-in-law against mother-in-law."

JOHN 9:39–10:18

9:39 And Jesus said, "For judgment I came into this world, so that those who do not see may see, and that those who see may become blind."

9:40 Those of the Pharisees who were with Him heard these things, and said to Him, "We are not blind too, are we?"

9:41 Jesus said to them, "If you were blind, you would have no sin; but now you say, 'We see'; your sin remains.

10:1 "Truly, truly, I say to you, he who does not enter by the door into the fold of the sheep, but climbs up some other way, he is a thief and a robber.

10:2 "But he who enters by the door is a shepherd of the sheep.

10:3 "To him the doorkeeper opens, and the sheep hear his voice, and he calls his own sheep by name and leads them out.

10:4 "When he puts forth all his own, he goes ahead of them, and the sheep follow him because they know his voice.

10:5 "A stranger they simply will not follow, but will flee from him, because they do not know the voice of strangers."

10:6 This figure of speech Jesus spoke to them, but they did not understand what those things were which He had been saying to them.

10:7 So Jesus therefore said to them again, "Truly, truly, I say to you, I am the door of the sheep.

10:8 "All who came before Me are thieves and robbers, but the sheep did not hear them.

10:9 "I am the door; if anyone enters through Me, he shall be saved, and will go in and out, and find pasture.

10:10 "The thief comes only to steal and kill and destroy; I came that they might have life, and might have it abundantly.

10:11 "I am the good shepherd; the good shepherd lays down His life for the sheep.

10:12 "He who is a hired hand, and not a shepherd, who is not the owner of the sheep, sees the wolf coming, and leaves the sheep and flees, and the wolf snatches them and scatters them.

10:13 "He flees because he is a hired hand, and is not concerned about the sheep.

10:14 "I am the good shepherd, and I know My own and My own know Me,

10:15 even as the Father knows Me and I know the Father; and I lay down My life for the sheep.

10:16 "I have other sheep which are not of this fold; I must bring them also, and they will hear My voice; and they will become one flock with one shepherd.

10:17 "For this reason the Father loves Me, because I lay down My life so that I may take it again.

10:18 "No one has taken it away from Me, but I lay it down on My own initiative. I have authority to lay it down, and I have authority to take it up again. This commandment I received from My Father."

LUKE 4:14-22

14 And Jesus returned to Galilee in the power of the Spirit, and news about Him spread through all the surrounding district.

15 And He began teaching in their synagogues and was praised by all.

16 And He came to Nazareth, where He had been brought up; and as was His custom, He entered the synagogue on the Sabbath, and stood up to read.

17 And the book of the prophet Isaiah was handed to Him. And He opened the book, and found the place where it was written,

18 "THE SPIRIT OF THE LORD IS UPON ME, BECAUSE HE ANOINTED ME TO PREACH THE GOSPEL TO THE POOR. HE HAS SENT ME TO PROCLAIM RELEASE TO THE CAPTIVES, AND RECOVERY OF SIGHT TO THE BLIND, TO SET FREE THOSE WHO ARE OPPRESSED,

19 TO PROCLAIM THE FAVORABLE YEAR OF THE LORD."

20 And He closed the book, gave it back to the attendant and sat down; and the eyes of all in the synagogue were fixed on Him.

21 And He began to say to them, "Today this Scripture has been fulfilled in your hearing."

22 And all were speaking well of Him, and wondering at the gracious words which were falling from His lips; and they were saying, "Is this not Joseph's son?"

JOHN 16:33–17:26

16:33 "These things I have spoken to you, so that in Me you may have peace. In the world you have tribulation, but take courage; I have overcome the world."

17:1 Jesus spoke these things; and lifting up His eyes to heaven, He said, "Father, the hour has come; glorify Your Son, that the Son may glorify You,

17:2 even as You gave Him authority over all flesh, that to all whom You have given Him, He may give eternal life.

17:3 "This is eternal life, that they may know You, the only true God, and Jesus Christ whom You have sent.

17:4 "I glorified You on the earth, having accomplished the work which You have given Me to do.

17:5 "Now, Father, glorify Me together with Yourself, with the glory which I had with You before the world was.

17:6 "I manifested Your name to the men whom You gave Me out of the world; they were Yours and You gave them to Me, and they have kept Your word.

17:7 "Now they have come to know that everything You have given Me is from You;

17:8 for the words which You gave Me I have given to them; and they received them, and truly understood that I came forth from You, and they believed that You sent Me.

17:9 "I ask on their behalf; I do not ask on behalf of the world, but of those whom You have given Me; for they are Yours;

17:10 and all things that are Mine are Yours, and Yours are Mine; and I have been glorified in them.

17:11 "I am no longer in the world; and yet they themselves are in the world, and I come to You. Holy Father, keep them in Your name, the name which You have given Me, that they may be one, even as We are.

17:12 "While I was with them, I was keeping them in Your name which You have given Me; and I guarded them, and not one of them perished but the son of perdition, so that the Scripture might be fulfilled.

17:13 "But now I come to You; and these things I speak in the world, so that they may have My joy made full in themselves.

17:14 "I have given them Your word; and the world has hated them, because they are not of the world, even as I am not of the world.

17:15 "I do not ask You to take them out of the world, but to keep them from the evil one.

17:16 "They are not of the world, even as I am not of the world.

17:17 "Sanctify them in the truth; Your word is truth.

17:18 "As You sent Me into the world, I also have sent them into the world.

17:19 "For their sakes I sanctify Myself, that they themselves also may be sanctified in truth.

17:20 "I do not ask on behalf of these alone, but for those also who believe in Me through their word;

17:21 that they may all be one; even as You, Father, are in Me, and I in You, that they also may be in Us; that the world may believe that You sent Me.

17:22 "The glory which You have given Me I have given to them, that they may be one, just as We are one;

17:23 I in them, and You in Me, that they may be perfected in unity, so that the world may know that You sent Me, and loved them, even as You have loved Me.

17:24 "Father, I desire that they also, whom You have given Me, be with Me where I am, so that they may see My glory which You have given Me, for You loved Me before the foundation of the world.

17:25 "O righteous Father, although the world has not known You, yet I have known You; and these have known that You sent Me;

17:26 and I have made Your name known to them, and will make it known, so that the love with which You loved Me may be in them, and I in them."

PSALM 109

1 O God of my praise, do not be silent!

2 For they have opened the wicked and deceitful mouth against me; they have spoken against me with a lying tongue.

3 They have also surrounded me with words of hatred, and fought against me without cause.

4 In return for my love they act as my accusers; but I am in prayer.

5 Thus they have repaid me evil for good, and hatred for my love.

6 Appoint a wicked man over him; and let an accuser stand at his right hand.

7 When he is judged, let him come forth guilty; and let his prayer become sin.

8 Let his days be few; let another take his office.

9 Let his children be fatherless, and his wife a widow.

10 Let his children wander about and beg; and let them seek sustenance far from their ruined homes.

11 Let the creditor seize all that he has; and let strangers plunder the product of his labor.

12 Let there be none to extend lovingkindness to him, nor any to be gracious to his fatherless children.

13 Let his posterity be cut off; in a following generation let their name be blotted out.

14 Let the iniquity of his fathers be remembered before the LORD, and do not let the sin of his mother be blotted out.

15 Let them be before the LORD continually, that He may cut off their memory from the earth;

16 Because he did not remember to show lovingkindness, but persecuted the afflicted and needy man, and the despondent in heart, to put them to death.

17 He also loved cursing, so it came to him; and he did not delight in blessing, so it was far from him.

18 But he clothed himself with cursing as with his garment, and it entered into his body like water, and like oil into his bones.

19 Let it be to him as a garment with which he covers himself, and for a belt with which he constantly girds himself.

20 Let this be the reward of my accusers from the LORD, and of those who speak evil against my soul.

21 But You, O GOD, the Lord, deal kindly with me for Your name's sake; because Your lovingkindness is good, deliver me;

22 For I am afflicted and needy, and my heart is wounded within me.

23 I am passing like a shadow when it lengthens; I am shaken off like the locust.

24 My knees are weak from fasting; and my flesh has grown lean, without fatness.

25 I also have become a reproach to them; when they see me, they wag their head.

26 Help me, O LORD my God; save me according to Your lovingkindness.

27 And let them know that this is Your hand; You, LORD, have done it.

28 Let them curse, but You bless; when they arise, they shall be ashamed, but Your servant shall be glad.

29 Let my accusers be clothed with dishonor, and let them cover themselves with their own shame as with a robe.

30 With my mouth I will give thanks abundantly to the Lord; and in the midst of many I will praise Him.

31 For He stands at the right hand of the needy, to save him from those who judge his soul.

LUKE 18:18-30

18 A ruler questioned Him, saying, "Good Teacher, what shall I do to inherit eternal life?"

19 And Jesus said to him, "Why do you call Me good? No one is good except God alone.

20 "You know the commandments, 'DO NOT COMMIT ADULTERY, DO NOT MURDER, DO NOT STEAL, DO NOT BEAR FALSE WITNESS, HONOR YOUR FATHER AND MOTHER.'"

21 And he said, "All these things I have kept from my youth."

22 When Jesus heard this, He said to him, "One thing you still lack; sell all that you possess and distribute it to the poor, and you shall have treasure in heaven; and come, follow Me."

23 But when he had heard these things, he became very sad; for he was extremely rich.

24 And Jesus looked at him and said, "How hard it is for those who are wealthy to enter the kingdom of God!

25 "For it is easier for a camel to go through the eye of a needle than for a rich man to enter the kingdom of God."

26 And they who heard it said, "Then who can be saved?"

27 But He said, "The things that are impossible with people are possible with God."

28 Peter said, "Behold, we have left our own homes and followed You."

29 And He said to them, "Truly I say to you, there is no one who has left house or wife or brothers or parents or children, for the sake of the kingdom of God,

30 who will not receive many times as much at this time and in the age to come, eternal life."

ECCLESIASTES 5:10,12—6:3

5:10 He who loves money will not be satisfied with money, nor he who loves abundance with its income. This too is vanity.

5:12 The sleep of the working man is pleasant, whether he eats little or much; but the full stomach of the rich man does not allow him to sleep.

5:13 There is a grievous evil which I have seen under the sun: riches being hoarded by their owner to his hurt.

5:14 When those riches were lost through a bad investment and he had fathered a son, then there was nothing to support him.

5:15 As he had come naked from his mother's womb, so will he return as he came. He will take nothing from the fruit of his labor that he can carry in his hand.

5:16 This also is a grievous evil—exactly as a man is born, thus will he die. So, what is the advantage to him who toils for the wind?

5:17 Throughout his life he also eats in darkness with great vexation, sickness and anger.

5:18 Here is what I have seen to be good and fitting: to eat, to drink and enjoy oneself in all one's labor in which he toils under the sun during the few years of his life which God has given him; for this is his reward.

5:19 Furthermore, as for every man to whom God has given riches and wealth, He has also empowered him to eat from them and to receive his reward and rejoice in his labor; this is the gift of God.

5:20 For he will not often consider the years of his life, because God keeps him occupied with the gladness of his heart.

6:1 There is an evil which I have seen under the sun and it is prevalent among men—

6:2 a man to whom God has given riches and wealth and honor so that his soul lacks nothing of all that he desires, but God has not empowered him to eat from them, for a foreigner enjoys them. This is vanity and a severe affliction.

6:3 If a man fathers a hundred children and lives many years, however many they be, but his soul is not satisfied with good things, and he does not even have a proper burial, then I say, "Better the miscarriage than he."

APPENDIX B—

GOD'S PLAN OF SALVATION

In America today, most people either do not know what it means to be saved or do not understand that salvation is something they urgently need. God's plan of salvation is good news only when we understand the really bad news; namely, that all of us have broken God's law and the consequences are eternally serious.[221] As a result of Adam and Eve's rebellion, something happened not just "to" them but "in" them that continues to have a residual effect on us — their descendants. It is as if Adam acquired bad blood that was passed to all generations. Our inherited sin nature places each of us at odds with a pure and holy God.

Without a *spiritual transfusion*, our condition will end in eternal death (hell).[222] Within the context of this bad news, the tremendous good news of the gospel is fully realized. Through the cleansing power of the blood of Jesus Christ, God has made a way of escape.

Because Jesus was God the Son, His death on the cross satisfied — made propitiation for — the sin debt for all people.[223] This means that the ransom price for your sentence of eternal death has already been deposited by Christ into your account.[224] Whatever amount you need to be reconciled to God is available to you through His Son — and through Him alone.[225] When you come to Jesus, He will require one thing — that you yield your life to be spiritually born anew in Him.[226] So how does one go about being born anew?

1. BEGIN WITH AN HONEST AND SINCERE HEART

God knows exactly where you are and what you think and feel about Him. Therefore, you're free to — indeed you must — tell Him the truth. If you're not sure God exists, tell Him. Then ask Him to reveal Himself to you that you may fully believe in Him. If you don't like reading His Word or you think His principles are too demanding or you don't

[221]**ROMANS 3**
23 For all have sinned and fall short of the glory of God.
ROMANS 6
23 For the wages of sin is death, but the free gift of God is eternal life.

[222]**ROMANS 5**
12 Therefore, just as through one man sin entered into the world, and death through sin, and so death spread to all men, because all sinned.

[223]**1 JOHN 2**
2 And He Himself is the propitiation for our sins; and not for ours only, but also for those of the whole world.

[224]**ROMANS 3**
24-26 [We are] justified as a gift by His grace through the redemption which is in Christ Jesus; whom God displayed publicly as a propitiation in His blood through faith . . . in the forbearance of God He passed over the sins previously committed; . . . that He would be just and the justifier of the one who has faith in Jesus.

[225]**ACTS 4**
12 There is salvation in no one else; for there is no other name [besides Jesus] under heaven that has been given among men, by which we must be saved.

[226] **1 PETER 3**

18 For Christ also died for sins once for all, the just for the unjust . . . having been put to death in the flesh, but made alive in the spirit.

[227] **1 PETER 2**

2 Like newborn babies, long for the pure milk of the word, so that by it you may grow in respect to salvation.

[228] **ROMANS 3**

10-12 As it is written, "THERE IS NONE RIGHTEOUS, NOT EVEN ONE; THERE IS NONE WHO UNDERSTANDS, THERE IS NONE WHO SEEKS FOR GOD; ALL HAVE TURNED ASIDE, TOGETHER THEY HAVE BECOME USELESS; THERE IS NONE WHO DOES GOOD, THERE IS NOT EVEN ONE."

[229] **1 JOHN 1**

9 If we confess our sins, He is faithful and righteous to forgive us our sins and to cleanse us from all unrighteousness.

[230] **2 CORINTHIANS 7**

10 For the sorrow that is according to the will of God produces a repentance without regret, leading to salvation, but the sorrow of the world produces death.

[231] **EPHESIANS 2**

8-9 For by grace you have been saved through faith; and that not of yourselves, it is the gift of God; not as a result of works, so that no one may boast.

like going to church, tell Him. Ask Him to help you through your resistance and to create a desire to know Him through His Word and through His people.[227] Whatever it is that has kept you from coming to God—pride, fear, shame, guilt, anger, disappointment, unbelief, lack of knowledge—tell Him about it and ask Him to bring you to a place of acceptance of His will in your life.

2. CONFESS YOUR SIN AND ASK GOD'S FORGIVENESS

See yourself among the all who have sinned.[221] Don't get sidetracked by focusing on your good points or by comparing yourself favorably to others—even to Christians. Don't confuse religious habits, such as church attendance or Christian service, with evidence of your own goodness. When measured against a pure and holy God, all human righteousness is worthless. Agree with God's Word that you are a sinner, and acknowledge your failed efforts at being good. [228] Confess the specific sins you are aware of, such as pride, jealousy, prejudice, intellectualism, anger, rebellion, or anything you see in your life that is unlike Christ.[229] Ask God to make you aware of any hidden sins and convict you of sin until you are truly and deeply sorry for displeasing Him.[230]

3. RECOGNIZE THAT YOU CANNOT SAVE YOURSELF

Understand that you need Someone to do in you what you cannot do in and for yourself.[231] You cannot save yourself, call yourself to God, change yourself, or even really believe in God by your own efforts.[232] In fact, you can't even desire to come to God by your own intent.[233] But this is great news. It means that any flicker of interest you have toward knowing God is evidence that He is calling you personally to Himself. Your part is to respond to His calling and to yield to His rule and reign in your life. You can trust Him, for He is interested only in your highest good.

4. WATCH FOR EVIDENCE OF CHANGE FROM THE INSIDE OUT

Don't try to be good. Instead look for changes of the heart—different attitudes, greater love, peace, kindness, joy that spill out in changes in behavior.[234]

Be intentionally introspective—the changes may be subtle at first. Be still before the Lord and allow yourself to sense His presence and His peace. Ask God to let others see changes in you as confirmation that He is at work in your life. If you sense no changes or see no evidence of the Spirit in your life, go back to God and ask Him to reveal anything that may be holding you away from receiving His gift of eternal life. Go through each of these processes again and tell God you will continue seeking Him until He enables you to seek Him with your whole heart that He might be found by you, according to His promise.[235] As you grow in your walk with the Lord, both your awareness of sin and your wonder at the Cross will increase.

Meditate on the Scriptures in the side columns. You may want to pray them back to God as your own words, from your heart. Be assured. He is waiting and He will answer you.

Note: When you pray to receive Christ, seek out a Bible-believing church for fellowship, prayer, Bible study, and accountability.

[232] **JOHN 15**
16 "You did not choose Me [Jesus] but I chose you, and appointed you that you would go and bear fruit, and that your fruit would remain."

[233] **JOHN 6**
37,44 "All that the Father gives Me will come to Me, and the one who comes to Me I will certainly not cast out. . . . No one can come to Me unless the Father who sent Me draws him; and I will raise him up on the last day."

[234] **2 CORINTHIANS 5**
17 Therefore if any one is in Christ, he is a new creature; the old things passed away; behold, new things have come.

[235] **1 TIMOTHY 4**
16 Persevere in these things; for as you do this you will ensure salvation both for yourself and for those who hear you.

APPENDIX C—
ADDITIONAL ROAD MAP SCRIPTURE REFERENCES

[22]DEUTERONOMY 28

11-13 The LORD will make you abound in prosperity, . . . in the produce of your ground. . . . The LORD will open for you His good storehouse, the heavens, to give rain to your land in its season and to bless all the work of your hand. . . . The LORD will make you the head and not the tail, . . . if you listen to the commandments of the LORD your God, which I charge you today, to observe them carefully.

[49]2 THESSALONIANS 3

7-9 We did not act in an undisciplined manner among you, . . . but with labor and hardship we kept working night and day so that we might not be a burden to any of you; . . . that you would follow our example.

[63]GENESIS 31

4-7 Jacob sent and called Rachel and Leah to his flock in the field, and said to them, "I see your father's attitude, that it is not friendly toward me as formerly, but the God of my father has been with me. You know that I have served your father with all my strength. Yet your father has cheated me and changed my wages ten times; however, God did not allow him to hurt me."

[124]2 TIMOTHY 4

5-8 Be sober in all things, endure hardship, do the work of an evangelist, fulfill your ministry. For . . . the time of my [Paul's] departure has come. I have fought the good fight, I have finished the course, I have kept the faith; in the future there is laid up for me the crown of righteousness, which the Lord, the righteous Judge, will award to me on that day; and not only to me, but also to all who have loved His appearing.

Kenneth Boa writes a free monthly teaching letter called *Reflections*. If you would like to be on the mailing list, call: 800-DRAW-NEAR (800-372-9632).

MORE GUIDES FOR GAINING WISDOM.

Pursuing Wisdom

Study the characteristics of wisdom and take a guided tour of Proverbs
that will help you understand biblical wisdom and its benefits.
Pursuing Wisdom
(Kenneth Boa and Gail Burnett) $8

The Art of Living Well

The Art of Living Well examines the specific ways we can apply wisdom
to our lives, showing us the fruits of wisdom in our relationships,
our jobs, our actions, and much more.
The Art of Living Well
(Kenneth Boa and Gail Burnett) $8

The Navigators Business and Professional Ministries

The Navigators Business and Professional Ministries helps business men and
women integrate and extend their faith to their families, their peers and their
communities. B&P staff use one-to-one and small-group meetings as well as local
and national leadership seminars to assist business people. Call (972) 931-8656 for
more information or visit their website at www.bpnavigators.org.

Get your copy today at your local bookstore, through our website at
www.navpress.com, or by calling (800) 366-7788. Ask for offer **#6058**
or a FREE catalog of NavPress products.

NAVPRESS
BRINGING TRUTH TO LIFE
www.navpress.com

Prices subject to change.